Hear what your colleagues have to say about The Wedge® and the techniques covered in *Breaking the Sales Barrier.*

"Partnering with The Wedge® Group has proved to be one of the best strategic sales initiatives Lombard Canada has undertaken. The Wedge® continues to be the only sales training we provide to our brokers because it gives them the proper tools to compete effectively in today's environment. Brokers who have completed the course continue to outperform the rest of the industry!"

Dean Morrissey
Vice President, Sales & Custom Marketing
Lombard Canada

"We have grown our business by 75 percent this year, and The Wedge® technique deserves a lot of the credit. The beauty of The Wedge® lies in its simplicity. It has taught our sales teams to be more strategic, prepared and confident."

Peter M. Vukanovich
President
GE Capital Mortgage Insurance – Canada

"A new approach that gets the buyer thinking. Sets you apart from the other agents using the same techniques the buyer has heard before. Randy is energetic and forces you to be different...definitely recommend."

Mike Boucher
Welsch, Flatness & Lutz, Inc.

"Randy has a gift that few people possess—the gift to teach and coach sales professionals to develop their sales strategies through a proven plan of winning. Randy provides them a pirates' lost treasure map that, if followed, will surely lead to the treasure of sales."

Jim Shoppa
Shoppa Equipment

"I started from scratch with nothing to lose. So when The Wedge® came along I decided that this was the way that I could make myself different from everyone else. Now, three years later, with a million-dollar-income book I have separated myself from everyone else."

Ed Coker
Higginbotham & Associates

"Using the 'Red Hot Intros' technique provided me tremendous credibility with my prospects, far better than mere referrals ever did. My closing ratios increased dramatically when I was personally introduced to a prospect rather than simply calling and saying I was referred by. . .

This business is about relationships, and these methods help me establish and maintain strong, credible relationships with my clients that last a lifetime."

Mike Buchler
Commerce National Insurance

"We've used many forms of training, but The Wedge® was the first tool that allowed my sales people to really look at how much time was being wasted. . .and that time was their most valuable resource! The Wedge® concepts move our sales efforts to 'results', not just implementing plans.

"When I have salespeople quoting from the book at our sales meeting, I know I have found a useful tool to improve their performance!"

Larry Koomler
Marsh

"The Wedge® is a great concept, and I guarantee it works! Do what Randy & Brian suggest and preach, and you can't help but more than double your book of business."

Tim Brady
Brady, Chapman, Holland & Associates

"At my previous company, The Wedge® was invaluable in aligning our company underwriters with brokers in the sales process. Together, we made more effective joint sales calls. As a team, we closed more deals successfully. Hit ratio's improved dramatically. . . 20+ percent."

J. Russell Smith
Division Vice President, Groups & Associations
Fireman's Fund

"We have been using The Wedge® strategy at Sullivan Curtis Monroe for the past two years, and our producers have adopted these principles to increase their sales. We have written well over $3,000,000 of new business commissions by following these principles. In fact, our agency culture now has a common theme and successful strategy to write new business rather than just quoting accounts."

Ed Shumaker
Sullivan & Curtis Insurance Brokers

"The Wedge® is not simply the best—it is the only approach that consistently works. The Wedge® gave me the tools to win like no other sales technique available."

Greg Acker
Sleeper, Sewell & Company

"Consolidations within our industry have brought about opportunities for independent companies. The Wedge® provided the tools we needed to retain and grow our customer base. Rather then selling on price, we beat competition with our competence to justify our strengths.

"At last, we can sell our company knowledge instead of just beating a price."

Howard Skolnik
Skolnik Industries

"The Wedge® Sales Culture is the most effective and efficient means of survival in the New Market Place."

David McDonnell
McDonnell Insurance, Inc.

"Over the last year we have been working hard to dramatically change our sales culture. The introduction of The Wedge® process has helped us greatly to qualify our real opportunities and identify our true service advantages over our competitors. Culture doesn't change easily, but the focus the Wedge® brings is driving change."

Jim Mangan
Amerisure

"The insurance business is hard enough, so do yourself a favor and cut through 90 percent of the qualifying process by utilizing The Wedge®. What more do you want in earning a new piece of business? The bottom line is more commission and less heartache. Thanks, Randy, for a proven and effective sales program."

Scott Gregory, Vice President
Johnson & Bryan

"The Wedge® is a unique and proven method of supercharging your sales. This is the wedge—a new, groundbreaking technique that can be used over and over again—each time with proven success!"

David Hartsell
Account Executive
Marsh Private Client Services

"Prior to using The Wedge®, I had a book of business under $500,000. Now, in only three short years, my book is in excess of $2 million! I can thank Randy and The Wedge® Group for helping me achieve these results. My hit ratio is close to 100 percent. I'm definitely a believer!

Mark Stokes
ABD Insurance & Financial Services

"Our firm aggressively embraced a sales culture beginning in '95 after meeting with Randy Schwantz. We realized our vision could become a reality by leveraging The Wedge® among our production staff. Since that time, we continue to utilize The Wedge® selling strategies within Higginbotham & Associates. It has resulted in a 22.5 percent organic growth rate, far exceeding $1,000,000+ new revenue year after year. . . and, in '95 we had no single producer responsible for $1,000,000 in revenue. We now have seven, with more meeting that benchmark by year-end! Thanks Randy."

J. Russell Reid
President & CEO
Higginbotham & Associates, Inc.

By Randy Schwantz,
author of The Wedge,®
and Brian Jenkins

Breaking
the Sales Barrier

How to Develop
Million Dollar
Producers

The
NATIONAL
UNDERWRITER
Company
PROFESSIONAL PUBLISHING GROUP

PO Box 14367 • Cincinnati, OH 45250-0367
1-800-543-0874 • www.nationalunderwriter.com

Cover and layout design: Jason T. Williams

Supervisor of production: Kimberly T. Plunkett

Copyright © 2001 by Randy Schwantz
The National Underwriter Company
P.O. Box 14367, Cincinnati, Ohio 45250-0367

ISBN: 0-87218-397-1

Library of Congress Control Number: 2001095014

Printed in U. S. A.

Table of Contents

Foreword

What a refreshing experience to read this book. At long last, someone has finally captured the essence of success in sales management.

For twenty-five years many outstanding producers and quite a few good consultants have shared with me their analogies, techniques, and theories about sales management. Each time it was intriguing and, to varying degrees, enlightening. Each time I learned something—about analogies, techniques, and theories. Never about process. Never anything that starts here and ends there. I was always open to the new ideas, always hopeful some magic formula would fall into place, but always disappointed.

Countless visits to countless agencies changed nothing. I met some of the greatest producers in the world and remain in awe of their performance and accomplishments. Each was very disciplined, driven, and intense. They only ate what they killed and, accordingly, each was a natural born killer. But never a trained killer. As a group they had some techniques in common but never shared a seamless approach to the science of selling. How could this be?

My quarter century of wandering also has caused me to meet many full-time sales managers. Looking back, maybe three were worth their pay. For a while there in the late eighties, hiring a sales manager was in vogue. It seemed like a good idea. Then I started getting questions regarding the point at which an agency could cost-justify a sales manager. What a challenge. Surely there existed a point at which the numbers would fall into line. Surely this performance curve would be the linear dream that numbers junkies thrive upon. Then the reality set in. If improved performance per producer is the benchmark of success, it is nearly impossible to cost-justify a sales manager—unless blessed with a dozen recently hired natural born killers.

All of this experience has led me to four conclusions. The overwhelming majority of agencies hire a sales culture, then modify that culture with every new producer. Fewer than 10 percent set and monitor any meaningful goals. Less than 1 percent enforce any kind of accountability. And, a full-time sales manager is a waste of money.

Until now the discovery of the Holy Grail seemed more likely than finding the answer to the largest dilemma I have regarding sales management. There always has been, and probably always will be, a substantial gap in the commercial production performance of average producers and that of producers in the upper quartiles. This is true even after adjusting for account size, region, line of business, metro size, etc.

That's not a news flash, nor is it the dilemma. What is most puzzling today is that the revenue dollars credited to the average producer are essentially unchanged from that of fifteen years ago. Granted, we have been in a soft market for most of that time, but the market doesn't explain away the fact that producers today are credited with ever fewer accounts. Such a disappointing phenomenon fortunately is accompanied by a ray of light: the gap between the collective performance of average producers and that of high performers, the top 25 percent, has widened substantially in recent years. Ten to fifteen years ago the gap ran around 35 percent of average commercial production. Today it is routinely 65 percent.

Why? Because they have great sales managers? Doubtful. Surprisingly few do. A solid combination of process, discipline, and accountability is the true answer.

And that is this book's breath of fresh air. There is a step-by-step process for the average agency and its average producers. Better yet, this is not a book about the composite experience of natural born killers. The authors are not into rebirthing or personality alteration as so many sales advisors are. They want to turn average producers into outstanding producers and, as part of that process, turn average agencies into outstanding agencies. They believe that a million-dollar producer can be created and does not have to be born. But they are not in any way out of touch with reality.

What is an average producer? One that handles a little under $300,000 of commercial revenue. Suppose this process can help your agency double that or only improve it by the 65 percent industry differential between the average and high-performing agency.

Don't expect the magic bullet or the seeming quick fix of an acquisition. Organic growth takes a lot of work, requires a lot of discipline, and dictates a lot of accountability. And it is well worth the sacrifice because organic growth builds agency value a lot more reliably than acquisition. With some bias I will say that the greatest single factor of survival in the past ten years has been sound financial management. With no bias I will say the key to survival over the next ten years will be sound sales management.

Accordingly, I would classify this book as interesting and worthwhile reading for any sales manager. And an absolute MUST for agency owners.

— Larry Marsh
President
Marsh, Berry & Company, Inc

Preface

In June of 1994 I received a phone call from a woman with an agency in Chicago. Her request was a bit peculiar. "I read one of your articles and liked what you had to say. We would like you to audit one of our weekly sales meetings. We want to improve them."

We agreed to a fee and set a date. When I asked her what was wrong with the current meetings, she simply replied, "You'll see."

I flew north to Chicago wondering what awaited me. It was Tuesday morning. The room was set up in a big horseshoe, with an overhead projector at the front and seating for thirty. The orange juice was cold, the bagels were fresh, and the coffee was hot. So far, so good.

People strolled in, grabbed something to eat and drink, and took their seats. I leaned over and asked my contact, why so many seats? She replied, "We include all our managers, department heads, producers, and owners." The meeting started promptly at 8:30 a.m. when the head of the accounting department put a transparency on the overhead and talked through last month's results. Next an insurance company marketing representative took center stage to talk about new products. He talked about his company's desire to partner with this agency to help each other grow profitably, right before making a plea for more new business opportunities.

The producer beside me whispered, "Some partner! He'll be telling our number one competitor the same thing tomorrow morning. This is a huge waste of time." I just nodded.

When the marketing rep left, the sales manager asked for success stories from the past month. Most people passed on the opportunity story until it got to Manny. Manny stood up and started talking about his heroic closing of a new account. A two-minute story stretched into twenty as he detailed the missing computer file and the last minute, down-to-the-wire proposal prepared by a virtual task force of collators. It was anything but interesting, not to mention self-serving.

Next we went around the room to find out what was in the pipeline. Several producers mentioned an account or two, and then we got to Bob. Bob was making progress on three big accounts. He might as well have said he was working on GE, Microsoft, and GM. No one in the room believed he had a prayer now or ever to write the stuff. This time, the producer leaned over and said in a low, weary voice, "Bob's been talking about these same accounts for two years. No one even bothers questioning him. What a waste! I could be out selling."

During the general discussion, one producer complained that she couldn't sell because she couldn't count on her CSR to take care of customers—which brought the customer service manager to her employee's defense. This was followed by a discussion about insurance companies and how unpredictable they'd become.

Ninety minutes later, thirty deflated, demoralized people headed toward their offices. The whole morning was gone—no productive work done and not one, single step taken toward closing a new account. As they filed out of the stuffy room, my contact said, "See what I mean?"

Boy, did I! Why are so many sales meetings like sitcoms gone sour? The boasters boast, the talkers talk, the whiners whine. But it's never very funny.

Sales meetings are supposed to help salespeople sell more, make more money, and be more productive. That's why they are unquestioned rituals, sacred cows in most organizations. Department head meetings, administrative meetings, and marketing presentations are necessary too. But they don't belong in a sales meeting! Sales meetings need to be quick and to the point—or there is no point.

I left that meeting thinking *it's time to have a barbecue! Sales meetings need snap, crackle, and pop—something CRISP, something that gets to the point, something that helps salespeople make money now. Let's roast that sacred old cow and find a better way!*

I started interviewing producers and sales managers, asking them what they'd *really* like to get out of a sales meeting.

PRODUCER 1:   "I've been a producer a long time and I've got a lot of great clients. What I don't have are good leads. I wish I knew how to use my current client base to get good leads and write new business—without looking like a peddler."

PRODUCER 2:   "I'm awesome at getting in the door. Maybe because getting in is so easy for me, I sometimes show up without a strong plan of action. I give them my best pitch, but I'm not great at strategizing. I'd like to have a way to prepare that would help me develop a real strategy for closing new business."

SALES MANAGER 1:   "It's expensive to quote on a new piece of business. If we don't get it, every minute and every dollar we spent is a dead loss. I'd like to build something in the sales process that would help us screen out accounts that we probably *can't* close."

SALES MANAGER 2:   "It's hard to keep track and keep score— like reading tomorrow's newspaper to see who won last night's game. I want a score-board that changes as the score changes, literally every time someone sells a new account."

In other words, what producers and sales managers want from a sales meeting are:

- Leads

- Strategies

- Qualified Accounts

- The Score

That's when I began working on what eventually became the CRISP (Continuous Rapid Improvement Sales Process) sales meeting. In CRISP sales meetings the order of business is:

- Red Hot Introductions

- Precall Strategies

- Submissions

- The Selling/Sold Board

In a CRISP sales meeting you can bring a question about a sales approach and leave with a strategy or solution. It's a forum in which a producer can find out what she needs to know about a potential customer or unfamiliar competitor before the deal closes, not after. And everyone's accountable—to himself, to his team, to the organization.

Then I began thinking about putting together the book you have in your hand. As a sales approach, The Wedge® is very successful. My team and I have trained thousands of insurance professionals to differentiate themselves from their competition, to use The Wedge® to oust the incumbent and win new accounts, even in zero-growth markets. But top producers largely practice The Wedge® one-on-one. From Maine to California, businesses are looking for a powerful way to supercharge the entire sales team. That's what my organization is about. We believe that giving our client companies a ten-to-one return on their sales-training investment is good business practice. We do it and we're proud of it.

This is the **HOW TO** book that pulls together what I've seen, heard, and experienced over the past two decades about the way agencies can grow beyond their current goals—grow all the way to huge. If you're an owner, sales manager, business manager, top producer, or someone who hopes to become one, this is the step-by-step, no-nonsense, do-it-yourself sales tool you've been looking for. No glitter. No groans. No generalities.

Breaking the Sales Barrier provides answers to real problems, not more questions. It's about quality processes, not abstract theory. Now you can take the best of the strategies behind The Wedge® to build a sales culture that can increase agency value, grow million-dollar producers, and put the "F" word back in selling—fun. You'll do it with less effort and less cash than you ever imagined. If not, send me your book and I'll send you a refund.

The Wedge® works!

When you've applied *Breaking the Sales Barrier* to your breakout business, share your stories of success with me and The Wedge® team at success@thewedge.net. We'll send you a free CD with special tips on becoming or developing million-dollar producers and *Breaking the Sales Barrier*.

– Randy Schwantz

SECTION

1

Go for the Solid Gold Goals

Go for the
Solid Gold Goals

I wish every agency owner had the guts to tell their producers, "Hit the ground running or don't let the door hit you in the rear. You're a producer. Go produce."

But many don't.

There generally is one big reason why they don't. Lack of VISION. What do I mean by vision? I mean a significant growth goal combined with definite ways to serve customers more effectively. Winners, producers, leaders—whatever you call them—envision a bigger, better future. When you are driven by *vision*, it excites you; it wakes you up in the morning; it makes you hit the ground running.

Try this test on yourself. Stop for a minute and let your mind imagine that it's three years from now. What date would that be? Write it down here _____.

There we are—you and me—sitting at Starbucks® three years from today having coffee. You're telling me, "Oh man, it's been a great run!" What would have had to happen over those three years for you to tell me that?

I say this with respect: If you don't have a clear answer to that question, it's time to figure it out.

I've been fired from some of the best agencies in the country. I can give you lists of agencies in which we've succeeded and in which we've failed. In these cases, what we brought to the table was pretty much the same thing.

What was the difference? Some clients had the passion to grow, the will to change their sales culture, and the stamina to do it. They had commitment and direction from the beginning, from the top. They had leadership. And . . . they had *vision*.

Small, medium, and large agencies have doubled their new business commission in one year. They've gone from writing $250,000 to over $500,000. Or from $600,000 to $1,200,000. Recently, a firm we work with went from $3,600,000 to more than $7,600,000. This is new business commission. These are real numbers. And you can do it too.

What's the secret? Three things—vision, commitment, and training.

If you know you really want to grow and grow big; if the revenue figure you've got in mind has at least six zeros at the end; if you've got some clear ideas on how you could serve your market better and gain market position; if you know how many million dollar producers you want on your team BUT . . . you don't know how to get from here to there, it's time to work on your execution.

Breaking the Sales Barrier is a blocking and tackling approach to growth. It gives practical, proven techniques that you can put to immediate, profitable use. I'm not saying it's easy, but winning isn't magic. Well-defined steps done over and over again lead to winning. In the next few pages, I'll outline processes and techniques that you can use to create a sales culture that spits out money. All you need is the vision, the courage, and the will to turn the page.

CHAPTER 1
The Cult within the Culture

*But it is not the part of a true culture to tame tigers,
any more than it is to make sheep ferocious.*

– Henry David Thoreau

There's cultured yogurt, cultured pearls, and corporate culture. So what is culture?

When I was a boy in West Texas, one of my favorite treats was homemade ice cream topped with Mrs. Ford's brandied-cultured fruits. In Lubbock, alcoholic spirits were not merely frowned upon, they were outlawed. Nevertheless, Mrs. Ford kept a huge salt-glazed crock filled with peaches, pears, pineapple, and maraschino cherries, all marinating in their sugary juices, slowly fermenting until the syrup turned to brandy. When those bright red cherries and that brandy syrup warmed my stomach, I'd get an adolescent buzz I can still remember! I also remember the sweet, fragrant taste. Bowl after bowl, year after year, the taste was always the same. The fruits may have varied, but the spiced culture in Mrs. Ford's crock was so potent that no matter what she added to the mixture, the culture penetrated each new ingredient until it developed that familiar sweet brandied flavor.

That's what a culture does. Cultured pearls develop with uniform shapes, colors, and sizes because the process and growth conditions are controlled. When you develop a strong company culture, the same thing happens. You can drop a new producer into your mix and, within a short time, she will be operating like the better producers on your team because the culture takes over. A sales-oriented culture motivates, initiates, and supports sales success. It sets the pace, integrates team members, and teaches everyone how to get things done. A strong sales culture almost guarantees steady, reproducible, consistent success.

I recently had conversations with the leaders of three very powerful agencies. One said, "We give producers a five-year time frame to develop a $1,000,000 book of business. If they don't achieve that, they can't work here."

Another said, "Our minimal goal is $250,000 new business commission per year. If a producer doesn't achieve that consistently, he can't work here."

Another CEO simply said, "Producers produce. If not, they can't work here." These gentlemen are the leaders of firms with phenomenal sales cultures. Although their goals may sound totally outrageous for your company today, their standards shouldn't. All three are saying *you must produce new business to work here.* It takes courage, commitment, and *vision.*

Winning is not a natural phenomenon. Neither is losing. People have been trained to do one or the other. Both are cultural.

A sales culture is an integrated system that transfers knowledge, belief, and behavior that makes winning a predictable process. Moreover, if you can create a sales culture as powerful, as pervasive, as irresistible as Mrs. Ford's brandied fruit, it will enable you to weather changes in personnel, carriers, economies, and customers. It will encourage and inspire when you aren't there. It will communicate your vision and drive your business values. And you will WIN more often.

To create a successful sales culture, you first must understand what a business culture is and how it works. Each of the following elements contributes to the culture within your organization.

- **Environment** - The internal and external market factors that effect sales and your approach to sales

- **Vision** - The "big business picture" that defines success for you

- **Goals and Priorities** - The big picture, heartfelt, five-years-out goals that say what you want and where you are going, backed up by annual "stretch" goals

- **Strategies** - The overall strategy for achieving your goals

- **Routines and Habits** - The daily, weekly, and monthly activities that support and encourage sales

- **Ceremonies** - The ways performance is acknowledged and rewarded in order to encourage further success and reinforce your overall business vision

- **Cultural Network** - The people and influences within and outside of your organization that can create or sabotage success

One of the winningest sports teams in America is a high school football team in Odessa, Texas. Odessa Permian is MoJoland. In 1960, only five years after the school was opened, the Permian Panthers won their first state championship and the dynasty began. Cheered by the famous MoJo chant, Coach Gil Bartosh guided his team to an undefeated district season in 1972. Soon Permian seniors let it be known that MoJo and Odessa Permian High School were one and the same. The championship sign overlooking the field celebrates each of the football team's accomplishments, marking their five-PAW performances, including one national championship, six Texas state championships, eleven state semi-finals, seventeen state quarterfinals, and twenty-two district championships.

Imagine yourself as head coach of a high school football team in a west Texas town. Failure is not an option. Virtually every man, woman, and child over the age of three wears MoJo T-shirts on game day and everyday in Odessa. Young athletes use the same play-book, training regimes, rituals, and chants from seventh grade through graduation. MoJo is a vital source of individual and community pride.

Developing a Winning Sports Culture	
Environment *What outside factors influence us?*	1. Sports today is ultracompetitive with year-round training, keen competition among young players, expensive equipment, and media coverage of on- and off-field activities. 2. Gate receipts and endorsements provide limited revenues. 3. As costs and rewards escalate, emphasis on individual victories, winning seasons, and championships increases exponentially.
Vision *What do I want for our future?*	1. Our vision is to consistently be the best high school football team in Texas and the nation.
Goals & Priorities *What is our most important goal?*	1. Our entire organization—including players, staff, and back office—must focus on winning the championship every year.
Strategies *What key strategies will help us achieve our goal?*	1. My coaches, trainers, and staff need to: • Nurture and retain talented players. • Develop sound training regimes. • Study competition and develop appropriate strategies and plays. • Maintain motivation and discipline, both athletic and academic.

Strategies (continued) *What key strategies will help us achieve our goal?*	2. My athletes need to: • Be dedicated, motivated and persistent. • Maintain academic standards in order to qualify for the team. "No pass; no play." • Train hard to remain healthy and fit. • Study playbook and competition. • Work together as a team to make big plays. • Maintain personal discipline and make intelligent on- and off-field choices.
Routines & Habits *What needs to happen regularly so we achieve our goals?*	1. Review game video of us and our competitors weekly. 2. Study and practice daily. 3. Train for strength, aerobics, and flexibility daily. 4. Maintain sound balance in diet, rest, and exercise. 5. Attend all team meetings.
Ceremonies *How do we celebrate success to encourage further gains?*	1. Give praise and encouragement on individual plays. 2. Put stickers on helmets. 3. Have pep rallies, media interviews, public recognition. 4. Celebrate after victories. 5. Give trophies and awards.

Cultural Network *Who/what will help to create success?* *Who/what can sabotage it?*	1. Coaches and trainers 2. Fellow players 3. Parents and family 4. Friends and schoolmates 5. Alumni, community, media, and fans 6. College scouts and recruiters

Win More or Be Less than Zero

Relatively few product markets are expanding. Even the technology market, on a steep, upward ascent for over a decade, has leveled off as penetration turned to saturation. Once everyone who wants a computer or mobile phone has one and pricing is cut to the bone, new sales depend on gaining market share by directly competing against other manufacturers with improved products or better marketing. That's the state of most industries today, including the insurance industry. To expand your business, you must compete—head-on, toe-to-toe—for a bigger piece of a known pie.

Such a market is known as a zero-sum market. Any new customer is, at the moment, someone else's customer. In a zero-sum market, there are two modes of operation—defend or capture.

	DOMINANT	NON-DOMINANT
STANCE	Defend	Capture
CULTURE	Service	Sales

Big companies with a large customer base generally operate in defense mode. Defensive does not mean passive! Large companies typically develop a strong *service culture*. By servicing their accounts well, they protect and defend their territories, customers, and market position. Big competitors price aggressively, advertise frequently, and dominate their marketplace.

The successful sales organization must capture new business by taking it from both large and small competitors. You cannot do it with great customer service and occasional referrals. Growth in a zero-sum market demands an intense sales culture, laser-focused on targeting and winning new accounts.

Everyone in your organization—top to bottom—must buy into the sales objective. Lip service and team colors won't cut it. The culture must truly change. Support staff must support; sales must sell; leaders must lead. Every player in a sales culture has to muscle up, suit up, and play to win.

- The Wedge® sales culture:

- Recognizes sales and service as the most important elements of your business

- Creates routines and habits to support the sales effort

- Rewards sales success

EXERCISE ONE

Use the following chart to assess your company's sales challenge and outline basic strategies for developing a strong sales culture. Try to think *out-of-the-box*, disregarding concerns about money, people, and time. Your resources will be easier to allocate once you have defined your goals and objectives.

Developing the Wedge® Sales Culture

Environment

What outside factors have the greatest impact on the organization?

  •

How do these external factors affect sales and our approach to sales?

  •

Where do we expect our industry to be in five years?

  •

How must we change to prepare?

  •

What is needed to be more proactive?

  •

Vision & Goals

How do we see our future?

  •

In terms of growth and creating new business, what do we want in order to consider ourselves successful?

  •

What goals are important in order to be competitive, sustain growth, and create new business?

  •

Strategies

Which ways of doing business will promote consistent and predictable growth?

  •

How should we focus our energies in order to develop new business that meets our goals?

  •

What do we need to be good at so that we can get the kind of business we want to have?

  •

Routines & Habits

What needs to happen regularly in order to support and encourage sales?

  •

What process do we most need to teach and ritualize in order to significantly increase our production?

  •

Ceremonies	
What can we do to celebrate success in sales and to encourage further success?	•
How do we send the message of what is important and what helps us accomplish our vision?	•
What achievements are worth celebrating?	•
How can we celebrate worthwhile achievements?	•
How often should we celebrate?	•
Cultural Network *Who can be relied upon to help create sales success?*	•
Whom do we need to be concerned about sabotaging success?	•

Strong corporate cultures, like Mrs. Ford's brandied fruit and the Odessa team spririt, are self-perpetuating. It is virtually impossible for anyone to work within a strong culture and remain immune to it. Such cultures are sometimes described as binary—ether you're in or you're out. You, as the gatekeeper, have a responsibility to control who gets in. If you make a mistake, the culture will find and reject the pretenders.

For one of my clients, I interview every sales candidate who walks through the door. I tell the candidate right up front:

My job is *not* to get you hired. My job is to screen you out. I'm like an underwriter trying to determine if you're a good risk. If you get this job, keep in mind that this place is like the movie *The Firm*. This will be your last job. The president and owner have a thing we call the Thanksgiving dinner test. If you as a candidate are not someone I want at my house for Thanksgiving dinner with my family and me, you don't belong here.

Companies with strong core values and business cultures typically take a long, hard look at everyone they hire. They are looking for candidates who are not only competent, but whose personal values mesh with the company's hard-core values. The interview process frequently includes some type of personality profile or psychological testing and almost always involves several levels of discussion with key people. These companies keep score. They compare notes. One bad apple won't spoil Mrs. Ford's entire crock. But if the candidate is going to wash out in six months (which she will do if she's not the right candidate), half a year will be lost, money will be wasted, and momentum will be squandered. It is faster and cheaper in the long run to invest the time (and perhaps assistance of an external consultant) at the outset, before a mistake is made.

Once the right fit is found, another almost universal truth in companies with strong core values and cultures is an indoctrination or orientation period. If you have a powerful company culture, it shows. You'll have no trouble reading the writing on the walls. It's a banner. Check out the bulletin board. Read the emails. *Atta Boys, Way To Goes,* and *For He's a Jolly Good Fellows* sprout like weeds in the well-cultured business environment. What you will hear, on and off the record, is an attitude. For lack of a better word, it's an attitude of elitism. These people, this team, have a sense of being special, of being superior to their competition. That all-powerful sense of having the right stuff makes them hard to beat on the sales floor. Their success breeds success just like Mrs. Ford's fruits kept begetting brandy.

Expanding what you, your sales team, and your organization believe to be possible, achievable, worthwhile, and winnable is the ultimate goal of a strong sales culture. Compared to the challenge of clarifying a driving vision and shouting your hard-core values, it's fun.

WEDGE

CHAPTER 2
Driven by the Vision

*The difference between a boss and a leader: a boss
says, 'Go!' - a leader says, 'Let's go!'*

– E. M. Kelly, *Growing Disciples*

A golf student told his instructor, "I play in the low 100s now. Could you help me take five to seven strokes off my game?"

The instructor gently replied, "Is that what you really want, just to take off five to seven strokes? I want you to forget about what kind of golfer you are now. Forget about how far you hit the ball. Forget about how you putt. Forget about how often you play. Forget about what kind of clubs you have. Let's remove the glass ceiling and forget about the past. Just tell me, what kind of golfer do you *really* want to be?"

"Well, when you ask it that way, I'd like to be a scratch golfer."

That's vision. It's exciting. It's motivating. It can get you up at 5 a.m. on Sunday morning for a 6:30 tee time . . . in the rain. The prospect of a little improvement has no power to inspire. But when you're chasing your heartfelt dream, you can't help but be inspired.

If you own your own business, do you really want 5-7 percent growth? Really? Forget about what kind of leader you are. Forget about how you are as a sales manager. Forget about the quality of your producers. Forget about your value-added services and competitive advantage. Forget about your carriers, your support staff, your line of credit. In the words of Tony Soprano, "Forget about it!" Now, tell me, what kind of agency do you want to have?

That's your vision.

Let's go back to that introductory exercise. Close your eyes, lean back, and propel yourself three years into that great future. Picture yourself at a national convention. You run into a colleague you haven't seen for years. During lunch, he tells about his agency and its steady growth. Then he asks, "How's it going for you?"

You smile and say, "We have had a one great run. Must be about three years ago now, we made up our mind where we wanted to go. Since then ..." your story continues.

That story about where you dream of being in a not-too-distant future is your business vision. Vision is a beginning with the end in mind. It may seem impossible under your current situation, but it's the first step in making your future happen. Hopefully, your vision is clear. You're no longer looking for 7 percent growth a year; you're looking to double your business every three to five years. You want a book of business that will get you into the million-dollar club—for starters. You've put your goals on paper and shared your vision with the people who will play a part in it. If not, the time has come.

General Electric knows how to develop people with vision. They are so committed to it that they invested in a huge facility years ago—their Worldwide Management Training Center in Crotonville, New York. If Yankee Stadium is the house that Ruth built, then Crotonville is the house that Jack built. Jack Welch, that is.

In April of 2001, I had a chance to speak at the training center. Before my presentation, the VP of Human Resources spoke. He said something that I thought was right on.

"At GE, we found out a long time ago that if you give people growth goals of 5-7 percent, they will jigger the system and get 5-7 percent. Next year they will do it again and again and again. After about five years all you have is mediocre growth and a very jigged system.

"That's when we developed what we call a Stretch Goal, 20-25 percent annual growth. Great leaders look at that and quickly acknowledge that they can't get there with our existing systems. So, they reengineer the place, develop new systems and processes that will allow and support their ability to accomplish that goal."

Do the math. A 20-25 percent annual growth rate means you are doubling the size of your company every three to four years.

The history of successful companies bears out what you may already suspect—making money is more a means to the end than the goal in itself. Enterprises focused exclusively on the acquisition of profits—from Civil War era military suppliers who provisioned the Union infantry with cardboard-soled boots to corporate raiders of the 1980s and their junk bonds—are remembered only in infamy. They didn't remain going concerns; they never planned to be. In the end, they victimized their competitors, their customers, their employees, and their shareholders.

Not so GE. Founded in 1892 by Thomas Edison and Charles Coffin, General Electric was a high-tech pioneer before there was such a thing. The company was born to market Edison's many inventions. The wizard of Menlo Park promised that he and his team would turn out a minor invention every ten days and a "big trick" every six months. The team submitted up to 400 patent applications a year. By the end of his life, Thomas Edison, as either sole or co-inventor, held 1,093 registered patents.

For more than a century, GE has remained loyal to its innovative roots. The company continues to invest heavily in research and development and is equally open to exciting new opportunities as demonstrated by its diversification into such a seemingly unrelated industry as television. (As inventors of the phonograph and kinetograph [moving picture camera], Edison's team would probably not see this as much of a stretch.) This aspect of the GE spirit is captured in its advertising—*we bring good things to life.*

A GE mission statement offers insight into how the organization can continue to attract and retain the innovators who develop vital new products, services, and initiatives. It also tells us how the company outmaneuvers and outmarkets their competition.

> *Become #1 or #2 in every market we serve and revolutionize this company to have the speed and agility of a small enterprise.*

Within the GE organization, the mission affirms the company's commitment to grow without becoming bureaucratic. It not only assures stakeholders that change will be a constant, but that the company intends to be quick and agile in implementing change. GE intends not to *just do it*, but to do it well. That's vision.

They Did. So Can You!

You've heard it a million times: If you don't believe you can, you probably can't. Beliefs have a huge effect on one's ability to imagine. In 1982, I did a firewalk with Tony Robbins. I got interested as I was reading *Success* magazine. On page 35, there was a black and white grainy picture of a tall guy with his pants rolled up to his knees. He was barefooted and on the move. It captured my attention. The caption under the picture said, "Tony Robbins has taken more than 35,000 people on a firewalk, an experience he calls, *Turning Fear into Power.*"

At that moment I told myself, "I'm going to do that some day."

Eight weeks later Robbins came to Dallas and I was there. One hundred and fifty of us walked on hot coals late one Friday night. We showed up at 5:00 p.m.; went through a few exercises with the world's best known motivational speaker, Tony Robbins; then took a break at

6:30 to see all the firewood piled up outside. At 8 o'clock we lit the fire. By 10 o'clock, low flames flickered over a bed of hot coals. At the previous session, we had written our biggest fear on a piece of paper, which we brought outside and threw onto the coals. Instant consumption. When we came out next, the coals had been spread along two runways, each about eighteen feet long. It was time to walk. One by one, we did. Nobody got burned badly, just a few embers caught between the toes.

Please don't ask me why I walked on fire. I hope you ask me what I got out of it. Here's my answer. How many people do you know who would attempt walking on fire, even with an expert like we had? Most people won't, simply because they don't believe they can. But we did that night and so have thousands of people before and after—up to 1,500 in one session. What I became convinced of from walking on those coals was this: "If someone else can do it, so can I!" Think of the possibilities!

So What's Stopping You?

It would be easy to imagine doubling your agency size every three-to-five years if you believed you could do it. The problem is, most people don't so they never allow themselves to have the vision. So let's take a moment and learn more about beliefs—how new ones are created and developed.

The best symbol I've heard to describe a belief is a table and its legs. The tabletop is the belief and the legs are the references or experiences that support it. Some beliefs are strong; some are not. What makes a belief extraordinarily strong is the emotion in the reference point or life event that forms the legs.

Imagine a card table and a pool table. The legs that support the card table are not very strong. If you put a little pressure on the table, it will collapse. But the pool table has six legs, each four inches in diameter and made of oak. A 400-pound sumo wrestler could dance a clog on it, and it's not coming down.

Let me give you an example:

Conclusion:
It's practically
impossible to
find a good
producer.

Belief:
It's almost
impossible to
find a good
producer.

Reference points:
1. We decided to train
   our own, so we hired
   a college grad, and
   she didn't work out.

2. We've put ads
   in the paper
   and couldn't get
   anyone good.

3. We hired one producer
   through a headhunter
   and had to fire him
   after a year.

In the example, there are three references, like a three-legged stool or table. Each has a significant emotional attachment because a great need remained unfulfilled while money and energy were wasted. To change the conclusion, you must change or supplement the experience. Other agencies are recruiting and hiring good producers every day. You must ask yourself, *If they can do it, why can't I?* So make your plans and act. Perhaps you can ask a successful sales manager in another market to share his recruitment tactics and mentor you. Or you may be able to identify a local mentor from a different industry. Make it your mission to find out how you can uncover the secrets of success and then learn them.

The Air up There

Your vision is your very biggest business picture—the view from 30,000 feet. The how, the why, and the wherefore cannot yet be seen, perhaps not yet imagined. If your vision doesn't scare you a little, if it doesn't make your pulse race and grab you in the gut, you haven't yet found it. If speaking your vision aloud doesn't open up your mind to new possibilities, you haven't found it. Good ideas are the spin-off of a great idea. Vision is that great idea.

It's never too late to sharpen and focus your vision. It's never too soon. Whether you're working on your first million or your next billion, a little foresight is better than 20/20 hindsight. Vision enables you to see beyond the present, motivates you to create what does not yet exist, and empowers you to grow into new roles and new possibilities. It is not a road map to success. But when you're driven by the vision, you can blaze your own trail.

Business Growth Plan		
Vision	Double Agency Growth Every Three Years	
Goal		
Strategy		
Routine/Habits		
	Producer	Sales Manager

As you proceed though this section, you should begin to outline your own business growth plan. Keep it simple to remain focused on the essential elements.

WEDGE

CHAPTER 3

The Competitive Environment

The breakfast of champions is not cereal, it's the opposition.

– Nick Seitz

As the man said, *may you live in interesting times.* Take even the most brief and superficial look at the insurance industry today and you will agree that these are interesting times. Deregulation and market penetration by financial institutions and the Internet are changing the commercial insurance industry dramatically and forever. How you and your agency face the dynamic changes in your competitive marketplace will determine if these are the best of times or the worst of times for your company.

Survival of the Fittest:
Where are you on the food chain?

How many agencies that were going concerns and your competitors five years ago are gone today? How many do you think will be left a decade from now? Will you be one of them? The I.I.A.A. has monitored and measured the market compression. From 46,000 agencies in 1992, we are down to 42,000 in 2000, with 29 percent of agencies surveyed reporting merger or acquisition activity in the past year. A full 38 percent of all agencies now fall in the jumbo bracket, $10 million and up.

It's changed my business too. Not so many years ago, my business was helping small agencies grow. Now I spend most of my time helping big agencies grow bigger and large agencies grow huge.

Never has the business maxim—grow or die—been more valid that it is today.

FIRST COMPETITION MAKES YOU SICK. THEN IT MAKES YOU BETTER

The silent partners in your firm's growth and success are your unwary, unsuspecting competitors. Since they will play a major role in all your Wedge® activities, you need to be aware of them. The size of your market and number of competitors will dictate how much about each competitive agency you need to know. At a minimum, you want to know how large your market is, how many real competitors you have, and where you are positioned in the marketplace. The best advice I was ever given about market analysis is this: If knowing something will change the way you do business, find out. If knowing wouldn't change your activities in any way, skip it.

Competition is a part of the sales climate that can become a major resource and your best sales advantage. If yours is like most organizations, you know relatively little about your competition. So learn more. I'm not talking about high-tech corporate espionage. Did any of your key accounts formerly do business with one or more of your competitors? Why did they fire them? Why did they hire them in the first place? Have you noticed any changes in the marketplace that form a pattern? Movements of sales or support staff? Big accounts won or lost? Price gouging? Or alternately, cutthroat pricing?

What you know about your competitors will help you select the right strategies and target the right competitors. Who is vulnerable? What common weakness is shared by all or most of your competitors—perhaps even by your own organization? What would you need to do in order to turn that weakness into your agency's strength?

Being *on top of* your competition means that you have already risen above them. Are routines and habits in place to share competitive information? For example, when you get a competitor's proposal, do you copy or file it so that the next time one of your producers is facing the same incumbent agent, he can use it to prepare? How would you celebrate a competitive tip that helped to close a sale? When you begin thinking about competition this way, you are well on your way to setting goals that will bring you profits, growth, and success.

ASSESS YOUR INTERNAL ENVIRONMENT LAST

When setting your goals, consider your internal environment—staff, time, money, and other limited resources—last. As you identify specific goals, you'll get a much clearer picture of what you need internally and what additional resources (if any) are necessary. When you build a true sales culture, your internal organization will look different and behave differently than it does now. You may have the same team playing different roles; the same resources allocated to different priorities. You may not. But until you set your goals and develop your plan, assume nothing. And never, but never, assume that you don't have what it takes already.

THE WEDGE

CHAPTER 4
Values, Goals, and Strategies

First say to yourself what you would be; and then do what you have to do.

– Epictetus

aving identified your vision, you've seen your business future. Your company values and priorities are the foundation upon which you must build it. Vision and values are the roots and wings of your success.

All companies have basic or core values—deliberately or unwittingly provided by the individuals who built them. These values become part of the basic underlying structure of the organization—like the inventive Thomas Edison deep at the core of the innovative General Electric company.

Most company values fall into one of these five categories:

- Customers

- Employees

- Products or Services

- Risk-taking

- Innovation

Take a look at the list. What is the priority order of these values in your company? How strong is your commitment to each? How are these values demonstrated, by word and deed, within the organization?

"Quality customer service" is a predictable company value, but "service to the customer above all else" is a stronger one and "heroic customer service" takes it to a whole new level. Many agencies built their reputations and fortunes on treating employees like family. But few, if any, agencies would rank innovation or risk-taking as a number one priority. Core values do not negate or cancel one other. In practice, values that are authentic develop a synergistic energy. The sum becomes greater than its parts.

Family Values at Work

The insurance industry may be America's last bastion of family-built, family-owned, family-run businesses. David McDonnell's grandfather founded the McDonnell agency in Memphis at the end of World War II. The firm rode the wave of postwar expansion and growth in the *New South*. In time, David followed in his father's footsteps and joined a financially healthy and respected firm. Solid, family values were synonymous with the McDonnell agency—honesty, reliability, integrity, stability, loyalty. Small wonder that McDonnell agency clients tend to remain customers for life.

At one point during the 1990s, the agency's meteoric growth threatened its internal stability. While no top producers were lost, rapid growth and systemic changes generated staff turnover of almost 60 percent between 1992 and 1994. The agency recommitted itself to *all* of its stakeholders—including support staff. Producers were offered an opportunity to purchase stock. Customer service representative salaries were raised, benefit packages sweetened, and an incentive program initiated. The sincerity of David McDonnell's intention to retain employees at least as long as customers was evident in the retirement program he established. The agency pays the maximum allowed by law into each employee's pension plan. It sends a message loud and clear—we want you on our team for the rest of your working life. Period.

The gains in employee stability have allowed the agency to resume a steep upward growth curve by cross-selling current customers, winning new accounts, and acquiring compatible agencies.

Business, like life, is a work in progress. Take the necessary time to look inward before moving onward. By knowing your company's core values and understanding your priorities, you are well prepared to begin turning your vision into a series of goals. As Henry Ford said:

> *Obstacles are those frightful things you see when you take your eyes off your goal.*

I don't sell 7 percent solutions. When I'm told an agency's goal for next year is to grow by 5 to 7 percent, I know one of us got the wrong number. A safe 7 percent annual growth rate may keep you ahead of inflation (just barely), but it won't keep you ahead of the competition. But chasing your biggest, hairiest, most ambitious goals is nearly as much fun as catching them.

Suppose your vision is to triple your volume of business in the next five years while increasing profitability. Believe it or not, doubling the business in three years is not an uncommon goal. Agencies that have a vision, a commitment, and a plan achieve it.

If You're Part of the Human Race, You're in the Race

You can bet one of your competitor's goals is to appropriate part of your business by targeting your current accounts. Remember the best defense is a good offence. Suppose you are in a zero-growth market. Your company is well established and fiscally sound, doing a little less than a half million dollars annually. You've decided you want to take your agency to the next level. You can grow in two ways—agency acquisition and account acquisition (acquired directly from your competitors through aggressive sales strategies). Your revenue goal is $1.5 million by the end of year three. With effective cross-sell strategies and improved systems, you expect to simultaneously increase your profitability. Now, that's a goal!

Such goals can be, are being, and have been done. In 1992 when McDonnell decided that the potential was there to grow the family-owned McDonnell agency, what he had in mind was doubling the business in five years.

No goal was more critical than establishing a true sales culture within the firm. The key factor was a cold-blooded decision to stop quoting insurance. First McDonnell began exploring the untapped potential of existing accounts. It was like mining for gold. Beginning from their commercial property and casualty base, producers began to cross-sell all remaining lines—personal life, health, disability, pension. Today the agency writes virtually all of the insurance for 70 percent of their clients.

Eighteen months into the plan, McDonnell acquired a small local agency.

But most of the expansion in new business was developed by carefully targeting the sales effort. If the potential was limited or the likelihood of signing a contract remote, no time or resources were wasted on bidding. If, on the other hand, there was an opportunity to leverage a relationship or drive The Wedge® between client and competitor, McDonnell's producers went to work.

McDonnell began 1992 with five producers. The plan was to add three more each year. But every time he recruited three sales representatives, two would make it and one would not. The transition was even harder on management and support staff. Growing pains were further aggravated by the need for automated systems. McDonnell wisely invested in new computer systems and technology. He tightened his recruitment, hiring, and training procedures—investing time up front to find new producers who were a good fit. He also strengthened the involvement and commitment of his support staff. He likes to describe his agency as problem-solvers for their clients. They learned how by solving a few of their own.

Consider the benchmarks this former $300,000 agency set. They closed out 1992 at $1.8 million. Five years later, that figure was $3.6 million. In 2000, the McDonnell Agency posted $5 million in commission and is on track to do $5.3 in 2001.

Because It's There

One may walk over the highest mountain one step at a time.

– John Wanamaker

Accomplishments that are impossible in a three-month window can be achieved in three years. Profits and success are there—if that's your vision. Each and every business day, you stand on a plateau, poised for a new ascent. You may temporarily lose sight of the summit. From time to time, you may need additional skills or equipment to move forward. But if you're confident in your goal and your vision, you will ask yourself "How can I reach up?" Your answer is your action plan.

Once you've got that big goal in your mind (and in your heart), you'll quickly realize that you will have to achieve a number of more specific goals in order to get where you're ultimately going. Those specific goals are based on the elements of the sales culture outlined in the last chapter: environment, vision, goals and priorities, routines and habits, ceremonies, and cultural network.

At this point, your business growth plan may look something like this:

Business Growth Plan

Vision   Double Agency Growth Every Three Years

Goal   Grow annual revenue by $1 million:

                     $800,000 in new business (new accounts)

                     $200,000 in add-on business (current accounts)

Strategy

Routine/Habits

                     Producer   Sales Manager

CHAPTER 5

Habits and Routines: Turn Strategy into Work

The reason most people never reach their goals is that they don't define them, or ever seriously consider them as believable or achievable.

Winners can tell you where they are going, what they plan to do along the way, and who will be sharing the adventure with them.

– Denis Watley

Growing up in Lubbock, Texas, strategic planning was my telling my mother *I'm just fixin' to do it*. My strategy was to avoid reprimand. My plan was to procrastinate doing my chores until I had absolutely nothing better to do or the passage of time had eliminated the need altogether. It's surprising how many businesses employ a similar approach to strategic planning. I can tell you from experience and keen observation, it was a failed strategy for me back in Lubbock and hasn't proved much better for anyone else over the years.

A Plan Is a Plan Is a Plan

Every moment in planning saves three or four in execution.

– Crawford Greenewalt

Putting together a three- or five-year business plan is like mowing the lawn or doing the laundry. It's boring; it's essential; and, almost as soon as it's done, it's time to start all over again. Successful strategic plans mirror the organizations that create them. Some are disciplined and detailed. Some are more concerned with process than action, some vice versa. One plan might be formatted as an outline, another as a spreadsheet. Some of the best strategic plans I've seen were written on white boards in erasable markers.

As a general rule, plans that take hours to read get put in a drawer and forgotten. Plans that are crisp, brief, and action-focused are more likely to get stuck on bulletin boards, slipped inside desk blotters, carried inside briefcases, and worked.

PLAN YOUR WORK AND WORK YOUR PLAN

I was visiting with a man from one of the great states that is strong on natural resources but short on people. Over the past twenty years, he has built an agency that dwarfs most. I've seen agencies one-third its size that couldn't find a way to grow in cities with more population that his whole state. When I asked him why he'd been so successful, he had a simple answer, "We're the best strategic planners you'll ever find. We make our plans, we meet quarterly, and we hold our senior executives to an accountability standard unlike anyone else." This man believed he could grow. He had done it before and he is doing it now.

Most small firms, agency owners, and business people will tell you it's almost impossible to find good people, much less good salespeople. This gentleman will tell you that they are hard—but not impossible—to find. He just works harder, looks a little deeper, and, not miraculously, finds them. Once found, he doesn't leave them to their own resources. He focuses their energies and time with a plan. The plan is not just written, it is worked and it is evaluated each and every quarter.

The last phase of planning is the one least practiced—sharing, evaluating, and celebrating the results. Pencil results into that plan hanging on your war room wall. Take the time to photocopy and share it. Make the time to celebrate a plan well worked.

STRATEGIC PLANS START WITH STRATEGIES

There's the rub. You must have a direction. Most annual plans fall into one of two categories. The first group is drafted so broadly that it is essentially generic. When you read it, you cannot determine the size of the organization or the industry involved. It is not a game plan; it's a prayer. The second type is so specific, so overfull of names, numbers, and minutiae that there is no perceptible direction or pattern. More likely than not, there is no direction.

How many times have you seen a movie that didn't know what it wanted to be—a comedy, a drama, a thriller, a mystery—so it was a little bit of all of those and not very good? That's bad direction. If you have six producers and each of them gets the job done in their own way on their own timetable, you're also guilty of bad direction. Instead of having an agency, you have an office that houses and supports six freelance entrepreneurs. Two of them may thrill you, and two could be adventure heroes; but, unfortunately, one is a comedian and the other an unsolved mystery.

If you want to develop a strong sales culture, you must establish some basic parameters about how sales (and business) are done in your agency. Call them standing orders, marching orders, rules of combat, rules of engagement, rules of order, policies and procedures, protocols—whatever. We call them strategies. They are the underlying ideas and concepts that allow you to move in one direction as a team. You probably have some already:

- Renew every current account

- Make two, ten, twenty cold calls a week

We're just suggesting that your current standing orders are not designed for the kind of dramatic, dynamic growth this book is about. And however many you have, your standing orders are probably freestanding and independent (rather like the independent-minded freelancers who practice them). They are not part of a complete sales system. The first thing doesn't necessarily lead to the second, nor does the second build upon the first.

To achieve your ambitious goals and your heartfelt vision, you are going to need clear direction and an integrated strategy. You are going to need strategy. You are going to need a coordinated, integrated, deliberate flight plan that gets you from the hanger to the runway to the sky and back to earth—safely.

Breaking the Sales Barrier is built around a sales strategy. In sections III and IV you learn in detail what these strategies are and how each builds logically and inexorably into the next. They include such basic tenets as:

- Leverage client base for introductions

- Develop a pre-call strategy for each business interview

- Use The Wedge® techniques to defeat incumbent agent

- Qualify accounts before bidding or quoting any business

- Track potential new business for accountability

- Cross-sell desirable current and new accounts

KEEP IN MIND

Setting a goal is not the main thing.

It is deciding how you will go about achieving it and staying with that plan.

– Tom Landry

So you've got a vision, a goal, and a plan. How do you turn right thinking into winning behavior? You make it a habit.

Let me give you an example. Do you look like Arnold Schwarzenegger? Neither do I, but I'd like to. At least I'd like to get more bulked up. On a personal level, that's my vision; how I see myself. There's just one problem. Well, maybe two or three problems. One is that I'm rather slim, always have been. Secondly, I travel a lot and it's hard to schedule good workouts. And third, I don't eat very well. You know about airplane food.

So if I am ever going to achieve my new body vision, I'd better change the way I do things. Unless I find a way to habitually work out and eat the right foods, I'll never look like Arnold. I can't afford to waste time, my most limited resource. So this is one way that I've learned to prioritize demands on my time—or yours.

Most of our everyday activities are more or less important but may or may not be urgent. Most people respond to urgency, regardless of its importance. To make the greatest gains in lifestyle changes and the workplace, we must put a priority on those activities that are important but not urgent. Focus on the twos.

	URGENT	NOT URGENT
IMPORTANT	1	2
NOT IMPORTANT	3	4

I've been traveling for ten years and, in all that time, no one has made me get out of bed, put on my workout clothes, and forced me through a great exercise routine. It's a two. Number one is getting up to double-check the seminar room, hang posters on the wall, fold name tags, and pass out workbooks. It wasn't until my back started hurting at the end of a long session that I said: *I've got to get in shape.* I asked myself would this be good for my business? Would it be good for my family?

Then I started reading *Body for Life* (Phillips 1999). There they were—all my previous workout failures but with solutions. I made the commitment to working out and eating better while on the road and at home. I added some new equipment to my home gym and told my staff to book my rooms in hotels with adequate workout facilities. Then my wife and I got on the net and bought enough protein powder to fill a warehouse (individual packs, easy to travel with). Last, but not least, I had a trainer write out a workout plan. So, my game plan looked like this:

Personal Growth Plan

Vision   Look like Arnold Schwarzenegger

90-Day Goal   175-185 lbs; Body Fat from 28% to 18%;
Waist 32"; Chest 44"

Strategy   Work out 7 days a week.
Eat 6 meals a day, high protein balance with carbs

Routine/Habits

Work Habit	Workout Reps/Schedule						
	Sun	Mon	Tues	Wed	Thu	Fri	Sat
Bike							
Treadmill							
Crunches							
Bench Press							
Leg Curls							
Free Weights							

Mealtimes	Sun	Mon	Tues	Wed	Thu	Fri	Sat
6:30 a.m.							
9:30 a.m.							
12:30 p.m.							
3:30 p.m.							
6:30 p.m.							
9:30 p.m.							

Breaking a Leg Is Easier than Breaking a Habit

We're all creatures of habit—bad ones, good ones, ones that are so automatic they're almost reflexes. If you've ever started a diet or attempted to give up nicotine or caffeine, you can appreciate the difficulty of replacing one habit with another. If one of your goals is to create a sales culture in your organization, your first strategy must be to establish routines around which new habits can form. Routines function as the underlying structure on which strong, new habits are based. Sort of a *first you do it, then you live it* mentality—like telling a child to brush his teeth morning, noon, and night until that routine becomes a personal habit.

Working life is full of routines. Many producers are loaded with them: reading the paper, checking voice mail, talking about last night's game. Then there are the more important routines—like where to have lunch and what renewals are coming up in the next ten days. When it's all said and done and the day is over, it's amazing how prospecting—finding new accounts and asking for introductions—never came up on the radar screen.

Communicating what's important to you, what's important to success, is essential to achieving your vision. Many agencies don't have a sales culture because they've never defined what's important, other than high retention. And so a lot of bad habits and watered-down routines fill the void. Even good producers will get trapped in providing *service*. A client calls and suddenly the producer gets involved in solving whatever problem is urgent, stealing time from what is important but not urgent (sales activities like prospecting, preparation, competitive analysis).

To develop a strong sales culture, YOU must identify the habits, routines, and expectations that lead to writing more new business and at a higher closing ratio. Sales meetings and most sales management tactics are little more than a collection of routines and habits expressed in an obvious and visible way. YOU have to step up and take the leadership role. Your vision defines what's really important, what's priority. At that point, you'd better be committed, willing, and able to do those things every day so they can become routine and habitual. If you can't or won't or just plain don't do it, you will not produce predictable top-line growth.

A sales culture converts strategy to work—theory to practice. Now your agency growth plan might look something like this:

Business Growth Plan	
Vision	Double Agency Growth Every Three Years
Goal	Grow annual revenue by $1 million:
	$800,000 in new business (new accounts)
	$200,000 in add-on business (current accounts)
Strategy	Develop Sales Culture:
	Leverage client base for leads/intros
	Strategize each business interview
	Qualify accounts before bidding/quoting
	Track potential new business for accountability

Routine/Habits

Producer	Sales Manager
Maintain a top twenty prospect list	Set team and individual goals
Schedule regular reviews with your top 20 percent	Conduct weekly CRISP sales meetings
Cross-sell additional product lines on all accounts	Conduct one-on-one coaching sessions
Provide competitive info/documents/ resources to team	Create accountability
Ask for three Red Hot Introductions weekly	Monitor progress

Routine/Habits (continued

Producer	Sales Manager
Schedule six new business interviews monthly	
Use precall strategy before each interview	
Wedge and rehearse every closing	
Obtain commitment up front	

All that's left is acquiring the tools to implement your plan. Read on.

WEDGE

CHAPTER 6

Sellebrate!

Make no little plans; they have no magic to stir men's blood and probably themselves will not be realized. Make big plans; aim high in hope and work, remembering that a noble, logical diagram once recorded will not die.

– Daniel H. Burnham

'll bet you still remember those little red, blue, and gold stars your primary school teachers used to recognize and reward your efforts. Does anything give you that same, warm feeling of applause today? You may never recapture the joy of youth, but celebrations and ceremonies to recognize success are an essential part of every healthy business. Not everyone is motivated by money, and even those who are don't share the details with their colleagues. Ceremonies of celebration recognize the achiever AND inspire the corps. Winning football teams don't sneak into the stadium. Take time to cheer, applaud, stamp your feet, do the wave, sing *Jolly Good Fellow*, or dance the Iggy. But make celebration another of your sales culture goals.

Times Square

Few things are more exciting than Times Square for the first time. Dick Clark may have taken you there every New Year's Eve since you can remember, but in person it's different; it's better. You look up and up. Lights, colors, animated ads, stock quotations, and headlines race past in a dizzy blur. And all around you beautiful people, sporting the latest fashion underwear, look down from gigantic elevated billboards. That's when you realize that if you want to be cool, really cool, New York cool, you need underwear just like that guy (and a six-pack stomach too).

Times Square is a pulsing, flashing snapshot of who's who and what's hot in America. What if the war room in your agency was like that? Big Times Square charts, superstar billboards, and up-to-the-minute news flashes of what's hot and what's not. That would be one wonderful way to celebrate success.

Imagine walking into the war room in your agency and the first thing you see is a huge 48" x 96" wall chart with every producer's name listed along the bottom. An electric blue stripe soars upwards from each name—a graphic record of sales to date in relation to the goal. You can't help but compare your results to your colleagues. It's a twelve-month marathon of a sales race and you're winning. Every month it's updated and you and all your fellow producers show up for a meeting in which the sales leader points toward the Times Square Sales Billboard in the war room and shouts, "Way to go Susan, you're s—mokin".

That's sellebration—letting everyone in the shop know exactly who's hot.

For tools to build your own War Room, go to www.thewedge.net.

Wheel of Fortune

Ding. Ding. Ding. Ding. The bell was ringing. As I looked up to see what was going on, all the producers and all the CSRs were heading toward the center of the office. That's where the bell was, along with the Wheel of Fortune.

I soon learned that every time a new account was booked, the CSR who worked with the selling producer got up and rang the big bell. That CSR would then spin the Wheel of Fortune. Every CSR's name was on it. If the wheel landed on your name, you got the prize. Prizes ranged from $25 in cash to dinner at the best restaurant in town. They all wanted to win, even though none of them were salespeople or producers. The Wheel of Fortune got everyone involved in selling, sellebrating, and being rewarded for new business. Surprise. Surprise. It works.

It's Summertime, Let's Play Golf

What do you do with an agency that starts off the year great, then goes cold for six months? The easy (or not so easy) answer is that you pick it back up the last three months of the year and make your goal. But if you're the one responsible for the bottom line, that's a heap of stress.

The president of one agency did the right managerial thing. He analyzed the problem. *All of my producers are out playing golf in the summer. So we have a great first quarter and make a lot of money, followed by lousy second and third quarters where we lose it all. That leaves everyone (me especially) sweating bullets the fourth quarter working to get enough new business booked to ultimately turn a profit. Is it time to draw a line in the sand or can a little sellebratory reward, a little pomp and circumstance, change the behavior in this agency?*

A LINE IN THE SAND

His first instinct was to threaten every producer. Stop playing golf in the summer and go sell or I'll fire every last one of you. But he didn't do that. Here's what he did instead. He created a contest to reward success. Keep in mind, the agency was losing money in those summer months. The owner determined what the breakeven point was for revenue booked. Then he announced the contest. He'd split anything over break even with the sales force. Just to keep it interesting from a competitive point of view, he created sales teams. The team that won each quarter got a three-day, all-expense-paid, weekend trip (spouses included) to a phenomenal resort. Golf. Massage. Dinner theater. Altogether killer!

BOTTOM-LINE

By the end of the year, the producers were competing to see which one would win the awards. The agency owner had solved the problem of the summer months. They became, at a minimum, breakeven. The super months then went directly to the bottom line.

Sold

Most people, even modest and humble ones, love a little recognition. But sales people love A LOT of recognition! Give your sales team a weekly dose of life in the limelight. In Chapter 14, you'll learn more about CRISP sales meetings. A small, but very important part of that sales meeting is to record on a large wall chart all new business sold over the preceding week. Make it a ritual to record those sales and make the most of the opportunity as a sales leader to say, "Great job!"

Spend a few moments interviewing the top producer. Get the scoop on how she made the sale. If you have a real modest producer, you might have to put on your Larry King hat and dig a little bit. Find out how she got into the account in the first place. Who was the incumbent agent that lost it? How did your salesperson Wedge out the incumbent?

Sellebration Summary

We celebrate our kids' birthdays every year, but we don't stop at that. We celebrate when report cards come out. We celebrate after baseball, basketball, and soccer games. There are a lot of opportunities to celebrate and reward good behavior.

What's the point of sellebration? Simply to reward the kind of behavior you want and expect. It's an opportunity to be creative, but your sellebrations don't have to be different, unique, or unusual. In fact, the most important thing about sellebration is that it becomes the usual and customary response to a job well done. Consistency and visibility are essential in your recognition of individual and team success. Find ways to sellebrate often, and your team will find ways to make sales grow.

WEDGE

CHAPTER 7

The Network that Impacts Your Net Worth

The country is full of good coaches. What it takes to win is a bunch of interested players.

— Don Coryell, ex-San Diego Chargers Coach

Driving Your Vision

Now that you've abandoned that modest little Volkswagen vision for a big, bold, brand-new Humvee vision, you've got to inspire, electrify, excite, motivate, stimulate, and energize all the stakeholders who form your cultural network. Your carriers. Your customers. Your family. Not just your sales team, but your support team. And their families. Everyone who is invested in your success is a partner. Everyone you omit is a potential saboteur.

Any CEO can shout, "Growth. More growth. Massive growth." And everyone within the sound of his voice will immediately divide into three groups: those who love the idea; those who are neutral and keep an open mind; and those who say, "Is he crazy?" That's anyone, any idea, any time.

When the big goals come from your head office, the intended audience will respond with acceptance, neutrality, or opposition. You can't grow a business with too many people in opposition. And you can't blame your people if they're not inspired, don't understand, or feel left out. You're their leader.

When average growth is not acceptable, and it's time to turn the money line toward the sky . . .

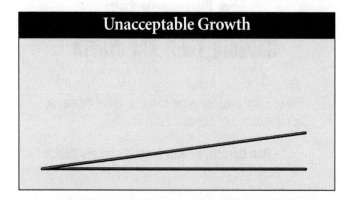

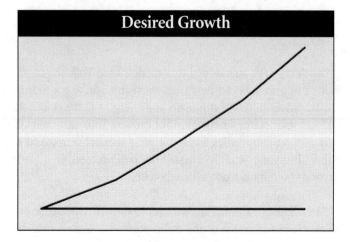

. . . that's when you look at your people and ask the brutal questions:

- Who's with me?

- Who's against me?

- Who's undecided?

At some point (hopefully very early in the game), you have to acknowledge that you can't get there without the people. You've got four choices, the top three are…

OSTRACIZE, HAMMER, OR GIVE UP

After doing the for me/against me analysis, you'll probably want to ostracize those people who aren't supporting your vision. (Let them have an office in the basement and send zero resources their way.) With any luck they'll leave and you won't have to deal with them.

Or if you used to be head coach of Pop Warner football, you'll just hammer them until they give up and do it your way. When they do what you made them do, you can bet the quality of their work will be unbelievable—unbelievably poor, that is.

If neither of those fit, you could just give up. Give up on your dreams; give up on your vision. Your favorite phrase can be "if only." If only I could have found the right people, if only producers were self-motivated, we could have grown a lot faster.

Guess what? None of these strategies works. None of them will get you the outcome you want. Your only other option is to **work it out**. But how?

FOCUS ON THE CUSTOMER

You can deny it; you can claim it's old-fashioned; you can insist that like the golden rule it has no place in business today. But the sooner you admit it, the faster you can grow. The customer is king. The customer can work management magic. The customer, and meeting the customer's needs, is the one idea that will make producer-lions lie down with CSR-lambs (or vice versa). Customers are the only part of the cultural network that can pull the whole team together.

Service and sales. They can be like a double-edged sword between your ribs. Producers who keep getting drawn into service issues are not making new sales. Not only are they unproductive in terms of generating new business, they are counterproductive. Producers aren't trained to, don't know how to, and are largely unsuited by personality and focus for good customer service. Chances are, when they get involved, they make the situation worse. And this really gets on the nerves of the CSR. The CSR feels sabotaged by the producer, so she doesn't support the sales effort. Pretty soon, you have a vicious cycle and slow to no growth.

You can tell your producers and CSRs to behave and make nice. But the only party that can inspire both sides to forget their differences is the customer. It is in the best interest of customers to have customer service professionals service their accounts. They do it best. And the most effective way for a producer to nourish her relationships with key accounts is to develop a proactive service timeline and stay out of crisis or problem situations. Establishing a sales-focused communication schedule creates a more professional image and makes it easier for the producer to leverage the relationship for introductions and cross-selling opportunities. In Chapter 17, we'll outline one such proactive service timeline.

Better Processes x Acceptance = Effectiveness

Whenever you want to initiate change, the first question to ask yourself is, *"How will this improve service to my customers?"* If you can't list a dozen ways that agency growth could enhance and improve the experience for your customers, you just aren't thinking.

Second, you need to identify the benefits of any proposed change on the people who are responsible for making it happen. Ask yourself, *"How will this help*_____*?"* (Fill in the blank.) When you have answers to those two questions, you're ready to turn idea into action.

Example: I worked with a group that implemented Goldmine, the contact management software. Once the system was up and running, management required daily updates of certain information for tracking purposes. As with most new programs, some were for it, some against, and the majority neutral. Those against it saw it as big brother watching over their shoulders, causing them to lose control. But there were some great benefits to both the producer and the customer. Management began promoting the key benefits of the program: processes that performed multiple tasks automatically for a group of people, instant reminders, central note taking, etc. As management began highlighting the benefits to the users, more and more producers began to come on board. But it could have been done a better way.

WORK IT OUT!

General Electric uses what they call CAP—Change Acceleration Process. GE learned early that developing a better process is the easy part. Gaining acceptance is often more difficult. CAP is a system for introducing new ideas, processes, or tools. It also can be used when something blows up and unexpected damage to productivity or morale must be repaired. GE's experience has been that the sooner employees accept new initiatives, the sooner the initiatives can generate tangible benefits.

Let's say you have a challenge ahead—such as introducing contact management software. You believe in it, and you want this important new initiative to get off to a great start.

First, put together a work-it-out team that represents all three groups of people—those for, those against, and those neutral. (Based on past experience, you'll have a good guess at how the chips will fall.) Develop a set of objectives focused on improving customer service and customer value. (No more missed appointments, last-minute renewals, misplaced phone numbers, or tasks that fall through the cracks.) Get a professional facilitator if necessary. (The highest-ranking person in the room probably will either dominate or pull back too far for fear of dominating.)

Make sure everyone stays involved in the process. Invest in value-added bonuses—like a preloaded database that includes your current clients plus prospects. (Target lists are readily available, as are database specialists who can slice, dice, and upload the information.) The form letters included in the system should be adapted for your industry and your market. Let the work-it-out team tell you which tools they want and how they need to be modified. Be willing to implement their suggestions before introducing the program. By the time you launch the new software, your work-it-out team has adopted it, adapted it, and bought into the concept. The rest will follow.

As you'll see in Chapter 17, The Wedge® says, "The best idea anyone ever heard was the one they thought of themselves." So lead them, guide them, show them the way to your great idea. Your work-it-out team will become the firm's cheerleaders for your new ideas. Because this process substantially shortens the time it takes to gain acceptance, your business can grow fat and happy faster.

Think about it like this: the speed with which you are able to accomplish your goals/vision is in direct proportion to the amount of acceptance you obtain from your people. This simply means that the quicker you can get those who are neutral or opposed to your initiatives on board, the quicker you'll reach your goals.

Obviously, your customers and employees are the most important part of your cultural network, but there are other stakeholders. Your carriers will want to share in your success. And families of your employees can be allies or agent provocateurs. Letters of congratulations or thanks, employee newsletters, and written recognition of the employee's hiring anniversary should always be mailed to the home address. If possible, invite the spouse or family to company holiday or seasonal celebrations. Rewards that give the employee an opportunity to include the spouse in sellebrations (dinner certificates, sports tickets, movie passes, etc.) also help to solidify family support.

For better or worse, your company's growth is dependent on the individuals you recruit, select, and hire—AND on a larger cultural network over which you have little control. The better you are at inclusion, involvement, and appreciation, the more influence you will have on both groups. Use the best of your leadership skills to help your cultural network maximize your net worth.

WEDGE

SECTION

2

If the Shoe Fits...

If the Shoe Fits...

People drive the vision, environment, goals, routines, and network of your Sales Culture. Those people—the ones you hired, the ones you inherited, the ones out there in the netherworld of the network, and the one that's you—bring unique sets of skills and talents to the party. They also have individual personalities, and each has his own personal reasons for being there.

In an agency, all the different personalities in the world fit into one of four distinct and necessary roles:

- owner/stockholder

- sales manager

- producer

- support staff

You might have aspiring artists, engineering marvels, budding entrepreneurs, financial geniuses, and family therapists in the mix. Regardless of what they once were or hope to become, while they work for you, you need them to:

- sell to customers,

- manage customer sales, or

- support the customer after sales.

  Th-th-th-th-th-th-th-th-th-that's all folks!

To achieve exceptional growth and success, all you need to do is to get a diverse group of complex individuals to meet your basic business needs. A few super-achievers and over-achievers would be nice to have. But if everyone would just do their part well, the results would be amazing! As you work toward that goal, remember that gaps and deficiencies are never in one area, one process, or one person. That's what makes the insurance industry so challenging.

Jeff Foxworthy made a mint telling Redneck jokes. My favorite was:

> *If the woman of the house says to the husband, "Honey, would you move the transmission so I can take a bath?", then you might be a Redneck.*

I've always wondered if Rednecks loved or hated Foxworthy. I'm guessing they love him because someone is buying all his books and tapes. In the following chapters, we'll have a little fun looking at agents the way Foxworthy looks at Rednecks.

CHAPTER 8
Owners and Blood Stockholders

For the most part, agency owners and stockholders are not rednecks. Because they are the lifeblood of the business, we see them as:

- Blue Bloods

- Hot Bloods

- No Bloods

- Cold Bloods

- Warm Bloods

Blue Bloods

You won't find a better person on the planet than a true Blue Blood (also known as old school or good ol' boy). They are the stuff of legends. They know everybody worth knowing. In fact, their social connections and relationships are so important to them that they "wouldn't want to mess up a good relationship by writing their friends' insurance. If they want help, they'll ask for it."

Blue bloods are on the boards of charities, nonprofits, churches, hospitals, rotaries, and just about anything else you can name. They are big on service to the community and the public at large.

But as powerful agency owners, they can be a little short on drive. And I'm not talking golf. In fact, their golf game could well be their number one asset. Mention changing something to blue bloods and they will say, "That's the way we've always done it." So they're going to keep doing it that way, all the way to being bought out by some bank.

Blue bloods hire other blue bloods. If they did hire a hotshot producer, they would run him out of town for fear he'd ruin the 100-year-old reputation their granddaddy established.

We love blue bloods as friends and countrymen, but oftentimes their clubby world is not a good place to work if you want to put the pedal to the metal.

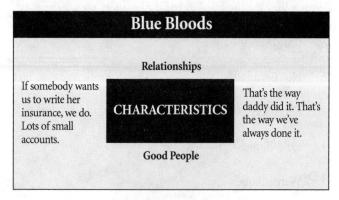

Hot Bloods

The credo of the Hot Blood agency owner is simple. "My way or the highway!" If it weren't for their temper and insatiable appetites for power and control, they'd be darn good.

When you work for hot bloods, you quickly learn to give in or be eaten alive. Let me introduce a term you might have heard before—

malicious obedience. That's when staff obeys and does what they are told, even if it's wrong.

Quick to boil over and slow to heal, hot bloods often live in the past. If they were betrayed once upon a time by an employee or producer, they still feel the pain five or ten years later. Having learned a lesson that they vowed never to learn again, they strive to maintain an ironclad, 24/7 control over every little thing. The bottom line result is that hot blood agency owners limit the agencies' ability to grow because they can't keep good people but can't do it all alone.

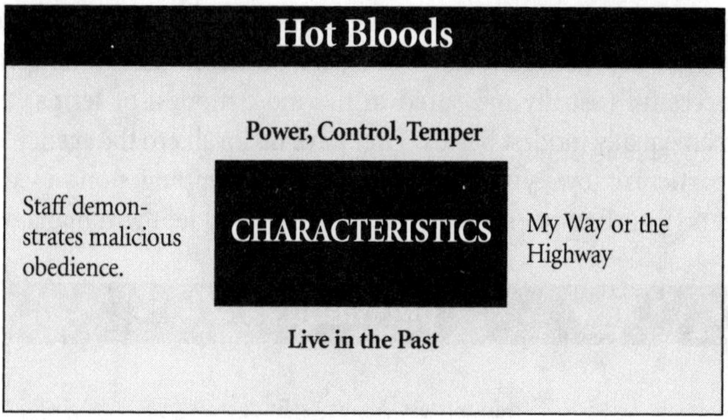
Hot Bloods
Power, Control, Temper
Staff demonstrates malicious obedience.
CHARACTERISTICS
My Way or the Highway
Live in the Past

No Bloods

Don't know and don't care. It's hard to believe that any business owners could be apathetic about their business, but some exist. They

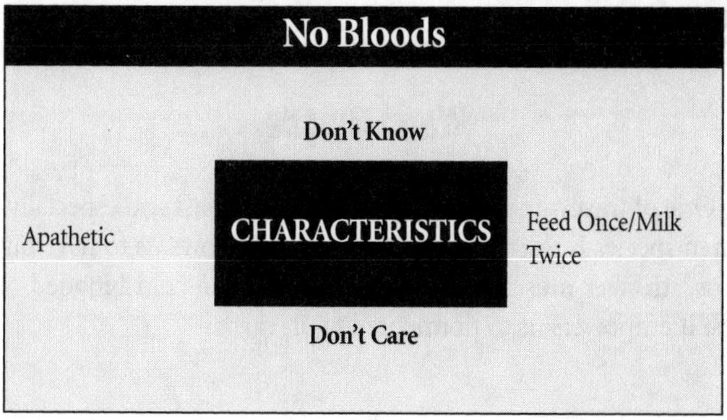
No Bloods
Don't Know
Apathetic
CHARACTERISTICS
Feed Once/Milk Twice
Don't Care

treat the agency just like an old milk cow—feed it once and milk it twice. What can you say except, "Have you ever thought about retirement?"

Cold Bloods

Historically, this type has been a rarity in the insurance industry. But every day they become more common. They are not owners, nor stockholders. They are asset managers. When banks and other financial institutions swallow insurance agencies, they fall under the leadership of asset managers. Some of them are administrators, some accountants. Some come from a marketing background. Some are secretaries on steroids. But none are invested in the agency or its success. They are managers, clock-watchers, beancounters. If the agency is successful (usually measured in the most modest of terms) they earn an equally modest bonus. They have no loyalty to the agency and no particular loyalty to you. This is just a stepping stone in their careers. Your best bet is to step out the door and let them manage.

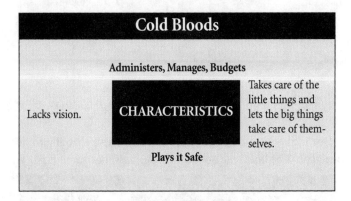

Warm Bloods

One of the evolutionary keys for all mammals and especially the human species is warm blood. Warm blood allows us to have bigger brains, stronger muscles, and greater speed than cold-blooded creatures. It empowers us to dominate life on earth.

Great agency owners are warm bloods. They are visionary in their approach and lead by example. They set up systems that reward success and have consequences for underperformance. Great agency owners never underestimate the need for a written plan and judicious accountability. The great ones have a talent for building a consensus around an idea and are willing to lead the charge for needed changes. They are motivators and communicators in their own special ways. They act and react in a human way.

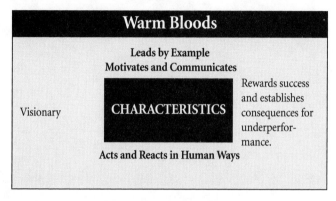

Warm Bloods

Leads by Example
Motivates and Communicates

Visionary   **CHARACTERISTICS**   Rewards success and establishes consequences for underperformance.

Acts and Reacts in Human Ways

Why all this Blood Work?

We used the terms Blue Blood, Hot Blood, No Blood, Cold Blood, and Warm Blood to create a memorable contrast between the characteristics of agency owners who make things happen and those who don't. The point is, Blue Bloods rarely establish a sales culture because the drive is not strong enough. Hot Bloods struggle because they run off good producers. No Bloods, well, you should call the ambulance, they're DOA. Cold Bloods are administrators, not leaders. But the Warm Bloods can, do, and will succeed.

If your goal is to warm up for a race to the top, read Chapter 1 again and then run on over to Chapter 21 on strategic planning. You'll get exactly the tools you need to get growing.

Vision + Plan = Hope

CHAPTER 9
Sales Managers

§ales managers have a lot in common with gunslingers from the Old West. At least it seems that way to me.

Just Shoot Me

The first type of agency sales manager is Mr. Big owner. Big book, big management, and big frustrations. Why? No time to plan; no energy to do it. And because his producers are content with their own $300,000-$400,000 book, Mr. Big has to keep building his own book to create income. Overwhelmed with all his responsibilities and yet desperate to grow sales, he delegates responsibility to . . .

Shoot Me, Too

Mr. Big Junior is the second type of sales manager. He is junior owner and gunslinger on the make. Junior runs into the same problem as Mr. Big. Junior is trying to renew his current book, sell new accounts, and, in his spare time, he's struggling to mentor, coach, and run sales meetings. He spends so little time managing sales that nothing much happens. He quickly sees that the effort he's expending has absolutely no financial upside. If anything, it's detracting from growing his own book of business. So he promptly resigns this prestigious role, which sets the scene for new blood.

Hired Gun

If they can still afford it, most agencies will hire an outside sales manager. The outsider comes in as a Hired Gun and quickly finds out there are two sets of rules. "Do unto them, not me," say the owners. So he's thinking, *I was hired by the owners to work with the owners to make them more productive, but they don't want to do what it will take to increase revenue. They just want everyone else—the employees and producers—to fall in line.* Since the owners hired him, he can't bite the hand that feeds him. He ends up working with the nonowner producers—all the responsibility and no authority. Pretty soon the townsfolk see him as the enemy, the bad guy who badmouths them to the boss. The outsider has no book, and, therefore, no credibility. In fact, it's often said, "If he could sell, he wouldn't have taken this job."

The bottom-line is that nothing productive happens, just like the past two guys. Within six to twelve months, Mr. Big moans, "We sure are wasting a lot of money on this outside sales manager. He costs me a bundle, produces no revenue, and sales ain't up either. Ain't he a waste of time." The hired gun is fired. Mr. Big steps back into the position. And the cycle starts all over again.

That's why being a sales manager is so hard. It's one of the hardest jobs there is. The reality is that all of these models are fatally flawed and most likely will never work.

No fear. Help is on the way in Section 3. Until then, read on.

WEDGE

CHAPTER 10

Understanding Producers

Being a business owner is tough under almost any circumstances. It's like raising a child. There are books on how to do it, just none that relate to *my* situation. Add to that the difficulty of trying to squeeze in some sales management and it becomes even tougher. Now, let's add insult to injury. Let's talk about dealing with producers.

Regardless of what underwriters say about producers, I think they're great—most of them anyway. Producers are as different as night and day. On one end of the spectrum, you have the professional golfer with an insurance license and on the other end you have the geek to the 14th power who takes home policies and reads them for pleasure. Yes, there are many varieties.

In my experience, there are four basic types of producers:

• You don't understand who I am.

• I don't understand who I am.

- I just want more understanding.

- I want to understand.

You Don't Understand Who I Am

Sales Manager:	Let's talk about ways to increase production.
Producer:	Look, I've been doing this for twenty years, I really think I can handle it.
Sales Manager:	I know you can. Could we just take a few moments to look at your pipeline so we can get a sense of your production for the next six months?
Producer:	Well, I don't work that way. I work off of relationships. I'm involved in a lot of organizations and when people need help, they know whom to call.
Sales Manager:	I appreciate the visibility and reputation you've created in the community, but certainly you've got a more predictable sales process.
Producer:	Look. I write new business every year and that's how I do it. How come that's not good enough for you anymore?

Well, there's nothing like having a "You don't understand who I am" around to write up a new account or two every year. But is that kind of growth good enough anymore?

How about the next stereotype?

I Don't Understand Who I Am

Producer:	Well, I just haven't got a good handle on the job yet.
Sales Manager:	Well, it's been two years, isn't it about time.
Producer:	Yes, it is. But I think it's just a string of bad luck.
Sales Manager:	What do you mean?
Producer:	Well, I've quoted on business. I just haven't gotten much of it.
Sales Manager:	Let's look at your quote log for the past twelve months. According to my records, you quoted on eight accounts. Do you think that's enough?
Producer:	Well, if I had hit them all, it would have been a good year.
Sales Manager:	But you didn't, and you probably won't. How much time do you spend prospecting?
Producer:	I prospect every week.
Sales Manager:	How much?
Producer:	I'll make five or ten calls.
Sales Manager:	Is that all?
Producer:	Hey, it's more than a lot of the other guys are doing. I've asked around.

"I don't understand who I am" can be fun to deal with. Too often, these people were talked into being a producer. They were immediately given a small book of accounts to manage or renew. To them the only hiccup is that no one in the agency gave them any more accounts.

I Just Want More Understanding

Sales Manager: How are things going?

Producer: Great! I'm having a good year.

Sales Manager: Tell me about it.

Producer: It's pretty simple. I cold call three days a week for ninety minutes. My goal is eight appointments a week. I meet with my prospects, tell them our story, and try to get to quote. I always ask before I leave, "If I can save you money and improve your coverage, can we do business?" So my prospects are highly qualified.

Sales Manager: Sounds like you've got it worked out.

Producer: I think so. I'm getting pretty good at this business.

Sales Manager: I bet you are. How much new business did you write last year?

Producer: I was proud of last year. I wrote $38,000.

Sales Manager: Really?

I Want to Understand
How to Do It Better and Faster

Sales Manager:	How's it going?
Producer:	Good, but it could be better.
Sales Manager:	How do you mean?
Producer:	I just finished my third year in the business. Year one, I wrote $42,000. Year two, $87,000; and, year three, $128,000. I feel like I'm doing well. I just want to do better.
Sales Manager:	Any ideas on how you'll do that?
Producer:	I have a few. But I'm looking for your help as well.
Sales Manager:	OK. I'll do what I can. Let's hear what you've got.
Producer:	I can already see that some of those really small accounts I wrote in my first year don't make me much money but can take a lot of time. I've got to start weeding them out. I also need to find better ways to capitalize on my client and other relationships to get bigger and better prospects in my pipeline. That's where I was hoping to get some of your help.
Sales Manager:	So let's talk.

The "I just want to understand" producers can make a sales manager's life a dream, no matter how long they've been in the business.

These producers are always striving to get to that next level, no matter how successful they are. When we hire them, train them, manage them, and work with them, we get better too. But how do we get more production out of the other types? It's coming, read on.

WEDGE

CHAPTER 11

No More So-So Service Teams

Although they are the backbone of most organizations, service staffs are outranked, undervalued, and overworked. They support a producer, a manager, or an owner who thinks the most important letters in the word team are M E. Yet when blame gets apportioned, they shoulder the lion's share. Time to invest? Guess who's at the back of the line? And while the sales team is enjoying a sellebratory lunch at a local bistro, the CSRs are taking up a collection for pizza in the break room.

It doesn't have to be that way.

Remember the Wheel of Fortune from Chapter 6 or the pay increases, benefit programs, and incentives that David McDonnell used to stabilize his customer service team in Chapter 4?

Customer service staff issues fall into some pretty predictable categories.

- I don't understand my job.

- That's not my job.

- Don't do my job.

- Job well done.

I Don't Understand My Job

Can you say undertrained? When was the last time your company invested in professional training specifically for customer service representatives on anything beyond telephone etiquette? Yeah, there was that time when the carrier's marketing guy came in and you let the senior CSRs sit in on the presentation—not the whole meeting, just the presentation. Plus you always let the CSRs have the leftover donuts. But do you involve them in the kind of training and goal-setting that you know is vital for producers? Do you share the big picture and your big plans with the service team so that they can feel involved, invested, and inclined to participate? Why not?

Your most successful and senior CSRs could help you map out an orientation and training program for new hires that lasts longer than an afternoon and would improve both retention and customer service. And they'd be pleased to do it. Moreover, they just might tell you what knowledge gaps they'd like to bridge and what ideas they could contribute to your agency's growth—only no one ever asked them.

That's Not My Job

The price we pay for getting off to a bad start is that bad inevitably gets worse. Lowly customer service representatives become masters of passive aggressive behavior. They don't lead a slaves' revolt . . . or need to. All they do is nothing—nothing that isn't written in their job description; nothing that they haven't been deliberately taught to do; nothing that they aren't specifically asked to do by a manager (or higher); nothing that requires initiative, imagination, or ambition. And guess what happens to customer service? How does that help when contract renewals roll around?

"Why," one agency owner moaned to me, "is it so hard for a customer service rep to ask, when they have the client on the phone on a service issue, do you have any other insurance needs? Why can't they simply ask if we can talk to them about their employee benefits coverage? Is that so hard?"

No, it's not hard at all. If you want someone (or some department) to feel like a part of the team, all you have to do is treat them like part of the team. Get their input and you'll get their initiative. Tell them where you're going and they'll help you get there. Give them an opportunity to solve their problems cooperatively and they'll cooperate before your next glitch becomes a problem.

Don't Do My Job

This is the biggest flashpoint in the agency—the producer *helping* to service the customer. It goes something like this.

Producer:	By the way, Sam just called me and said he got a new vehicle that we need to add to his policy. I was in my car at the time and wrote down the number the best I could. Here it is. If you could get this done today, I'd really appreciate it.
CSR:	Why didn't you just have him call me? It goes faster when I talk to him directly.
Producer:	I had him on the phone already. And he's such a busy guy, I hate to waste his time. If you would just go ahead a process the endorsement, I'd consider it a personal favor.
CSR:	Okay. But, looking at this note, there are only ten digits. A VIN number should have thirteen.

| Producer: | Sorry. Go ahead and give him a call and get the rest of the numbers. Thanks. |

The service representative may need several days and a half-dozen phone calls to get the correct information and process the endorsement. It could have been a five-minute job—for the agency and the customer—if the call had been directed to the right party. The producer could have made it easy for the customer by distributing a business card with the service contact name and number. He could have made the customer feel comfortable dealing with the agency team instead of just the producer. He didn't. When customers turn to the sales rep for service needs, it undermines the effectiveness of customer service.

Ultimately, if someone has to clean up after the producer (as they did in this case), it hurts his relationship with the client too.

Job Well Done

Agencies go to extremes to motivate and reward producers. Bring just a little of that attention and money to the service area. Whether you choose to incentivise CSRs individually or collectively, a small commission or financial stake in sales success is the swiftest, surest path to enthusiastic cooperation in retaining and cross-selling current accounts.

WEDGE

SECTION

3

Growing a Sales Culture: It's Not Luck and It's Not Rocket Science

Growing a Sales Culture: It's Not Luck and It's Not Rocket Science

There is no perfect agency. No agency that I have seen or heard about has perfect leaders, managers, producers, and support staff. And yet I've seen many, many successful agencies in which flawed people have put their own imperfections aside and focused on their vision and goals.

In this section, we're going to get down to work. We're going to work on the questions that you want answered. How can you take that vision we talked about in the very first chapter and turn it into action with a simple strategic plan? Taking into account the foibles, personalities, and different points of view of owners and producers, how can you solve the problem of sales management? How do you create sales meetings that squeeze money out of producers like slot machines?

Yes, this section is about work. But it'll be fun because it's packed with solutions that make sense and money.

CHAPTER 12

Down to Business

You gotta be careful if you don't know where you're going, because you might not get there.

– Yogi Berra

After being in business for several years, I was frustrated that even as my sales training program, The Wedge®, was becoming more widely known, it wasn't getting any easier to get new business. Worse yet, my revenues didn't seem to be growing at the pace I had hoped. What frustrated me even more was that, while my seminars were successful and evaluations high, the training itself was being poorly utilized after the fact. I was working myself to death and divorce. My staff was disheartened and disenchanted. Why wasn't my business getting any bigger?

Finally, it occurred to me that I was expecting the results to come without setting out in a deliberate way to make them happen. No wonder my staff couldn't make me happy. They didn't know where I wanted them to go. I didn't know myself. I knew that I had a gang-buster sales-training program. I knew that I loved conducting training sessions and that the participants liked attending my seminars. Some of them were making money putting the lessons to work because they wrote me to tell me so. There I was working hard to deliver a good product, and the big success I was hoping for still wasn't happening. I guess I really believed that, since I had built a better mousetrap, the world would beat a path to my door. The world did not.

I needed a plan.

So I pulled my key staff together and we began writing words on a big white board. We added and subtracted and fidgeted around with the alphabet of possibilities until we arrived at a simple, clear, understandable vision—*to provide training that works and to make it work.*

Some funny things happened during this process. First—all of us, all of a sudden, almost all at once—knew what we were going after.

After we identified all the obstacles and laid out what we had to do to achieve the vision, we experienced a second lightning bolt of instant wisdom. We came to realize that we never would have gotten there working the way we were working, no matter how hard we had worked. We were only doing the first half. We were focusing on a training event, hoping to create magical change within an organization. In order to effect change, the process had to be deeper and ongoing. We had to change the way we thought and the way we worked with clients. Only then could we *make it work.*

What Is a Strategic Plan?

So what is a strategic plan, really? It's taking your vision and values and giving them life. Planning is the action that takes your vision beyond a plaque nailed to the office wall. Saying is not a substitute for doing. It's the prelude.

A good plan will require getting down to business in these ways:

Drill Down - Be specific

Write Down - Blueprint

Get Down – On your bad self (accountability)

Drill Down

One of the major problems with most strategic plans is that they are too general and full of what we like to call "pooge." What is pooge? Pooge is words that fill space.

Newspapers come together in a handful of frantic minutes just before the deadline. As the editors review page layouts, there are holes. Space with no ads, no copy. Dead air. That's when the editor reaches into a file called filler. Filler is material that was not considered important enough to be allotted space the first time around. It usually is not time sensitive. In other words, it's information that is interesting to read but that you really don't need to know today, tomorrow, or ever. It's pooge.

Many companies fluff out their strategic plans with pooge—ideas and tactics that sound interesting but that no one really intends to implement. Your plan should contain only specific, actionable items that clearly lead to the goal line. Each new initiative will need a champion, a budget, and a timeline. If no one owns it, no one funds it, and there is no particular timeframe for accomplishing it. Guess what? It's pooge.

THE TEAM

Begin the strategic planning process by identifying your team. In addition to the owners and stockholders, your planning team should include the leader of each department or business unit, depending on how you have structured your agency.

THE PLACE

When my wife and I need some quality time together, it never seems to work out. First of all, we have four daughters. At least one is vying for our attention at any given time. But even if we were to get them off to bed or out with their grandmother, there are horses to feed and always something to fix around the house. Not to mention the fact that my office is on the property. All in all, it's just too hard to focus on each other at home. So when we really want to spend time with each other, we go away.

For similar reasons, the typical strategic planning session is an out-of-office experience. It may be a long weekend that combines team activities and recreation with rounds of planning activities—a two-day marathon or a single-day session. Leaving the office for the purpose of planning—no cells or pagers permitted—forces participants to concentrate on the task. It is the best way for management to send the message that this is important.

One agency I work with does its annual strategic planning at a local lakeside resort. The key players bring their families along to enjoy some recreation and relaxation during the work sessions. The larger group enjoys shared meals and evening activities. This innovative approach allows key players to focus on work-related tasks without compromising family life. It also is an interesting way to get support and buy-in from that cultural network out there on the sidelines. When work time intrudes on family time, it can create resentments and guilt. Allowing family members to see themselves as part of a larger team, and as part of the overall success of the organization, sets the tone for a climate of cooperation and support.

THE TIME

Meet at least annually. It also makes sense to hold informal quarterly or semiannual updates to see how things are going and to make necessary adjustments. Planning without follow-up is like setting goals without accountability. It doesn't do much for the bottom line.

SWOT ANALYSIS

A tried and true starting place is a SWOT analysis. SWOT is the acronym for a list of the following:

- strengths

- weaknesses

- opportunities

- threats

Invest time to identify these essentials because they will help you create a pooge-free blueprint for success.

Write Down

Setting a goal is not the main thing.

It is deciding how you will go about achieving it and staying with that plan.

— Tom Landry

A common theme we found among those companies that actually had a written plan in place was this: the plan was specific on a corporate level but not on an individual level. Even when employees knew the overall company goal, they were left to their own devices to figure out where they fit in the plan and what they had to do to make the vision happen. This can be overwhelming and, if you have no idea where to start, paralyzing. Work together to create a clear path for everyone to travel. This will help to guarantee the outcome and certainly make the process less stressful and more enjoyable for all.

Remember: general is a good place to start but a bad place to finish. A football coach wouldn't think of showing up for a game without a playbook. And he wouldn't let the players pick their positions and figure out what they needed to do on their own. They practice together as a team, each playing a different role, to prepare for one outcome—TO WIN. To win at selling, you need a strategic plan. And you need a team of players that understands roles and responsibilities.

Your working blueprint should include:

• Specific goals

• Actions to achieve each goal

• Timetable

• Responsible party

• Budget

• Results

Successful strategic plans mirror the organizations that create them. Some are disciplined and detailed. Some are more concerned with process than action, some vice versa. One plan might be formatted as an outline, another as a spreadsheet. Some of the best strategic plans I've seen were developed on white boards with erasable markers.

The point is that good plans differ in much the same way that their organizations differ. The strategic plans for my company and yours will not and should not look the same.

No matter how you do it, write it down. You wouldn't remember the time and place of all your appointments without a calendar. Don't expect your team to remember the play-by-play unless you write it down. Plans that take hours to read get put in a drawer and forgotten. Plans that are crisp, brief, and to the point are more likely to get stuck on bulletin boards, slipped inside desk blotters, carried inside briefcases, and worked. What gets written and gets read gets remembered and gets done.

Get Down

Remember the man from Chapter 5. He attributed his agency's phenomenal growth in a small western state to strategic planning.

"We make our plans. We meet quarterly. And we hold our senior executives to an accountability standard unlike anyone else." He focuses his team's energies with a plan that is not just written but worked; not just worked but evaluated each and every quarter.

On our web page, www.thewedge.net, are several formats that have been used successfully by other companies for strategic planning. Feel free to adapt and modify any of them to suit your own organization.

> *The reason most people never reach their goals is that they don't define them, or ever seriously consider them as believable or achievable.*

> *Winners can tell you where they are going, what they plan to do along the way, and who will be sharing the adventure with them.*

> **– Denis Watley**

CHAPTER 13

Team Sales Management

Good leaders make people feel that they're at the very heart of things, not at the periphery. Everyone feels that he or she makes a difference to the success of the organization.

When that happens people feel centered and that gives their work meaning.

– Warren Bennis

One very successful agency on the West Coast has a 79 percent closing ratio. Mr. Big Junior is the appointed sales manager. He loves working with the producers while growing his own book. The agency has grown an impressive 15-20 percent annually over the last five years and now tops out at $12 million in revenue. Not bad by anyone's standards . . . almost.

For every strength there is a corresponding weakness. Although this sales manager is great at helping his top producers develop winning strategies on large accounts (to the tune of 79 percent closing), he is equally bad at managing the pipeline. He does a poor job of holding the weaker players accountable. He hates playing traffic cop and enforcer. It makes him uncomfortable to post new business numbers on the wall for everyone to see. As a result, even though the agency continues to meet its new business goals and sustain a high closing ratio, this guy gets trashed by some of his senior partners.

Toughest Job in the World

I happen to believe that sales management is one of the toughest jobs in the world. The sales manager is invariably the monkey in the middle between a team of egotistical producers who want to get rich quickly and easily and an egomaniacal owner who wants the same. It's a position supercharged with responsibility for the top line of the business, yet under-equipped in terms of authority. The sales manager can play every card he's dealt with strategy, courage, and cunning, only to be trumped by the owner's ace. But I'm not telling you anything you don't already know.

Seldom have I met anyone who was truly equipped to be the sales manager. Why? Great sales management within an agency environment requires the following characteristics and skills all in a single human being: vision, leadership, coaching/mentoring, accountability, follow-through, system and process orientation, creativity, and flexibility. To me that's like watching Reggie White do back flips on the balance beam. It's an achievement to be great in one of those areas. But it's asking more than a lot to expect anyone to perform well right across the board.

DO WHAT YOU DO BEST AND DELEGATE THE REST

Individuals must overcome three obstacles to achieve great sales management—time, talent, and owners. Unless you are willing to give an outside sales manager the authority and resources to make a difference (which very few are), you are condemned to mediocrity. Worst case scenario is an outside sales manager who is little more than a highly paid babysitter and yet another management problem for the agency owner.

That said, your only other option is to look inside the agency for a solution.

First off, no sales professional worth his salt has much time to dedicate to sales management. This simply means that you have to spread the duties among several people rather than dumping it all on one person.

Second, no one person has all the necessary talents to do a great job. So your next step is to identify the different skills required, locate the best example of that skill or strength among the individuals on your staff (remembering that they need not all be producers), and make your match.

Third, and equally important, anyone who owns even one share of stock firmly believes they are permanently exempt from being forced to make any behavioral changes that would help them sell more effectively. To counter this powerful and pervasive attitude, you must have your most formidable owner/stockholder on the sales management team. And I mean ON THE TEAM. No backbenchers or Monday morning quarterbacks need apply.

Now, rather than trying to find one superman to do it all, you have a whole group of superheroes, respected experts in their own areas—a sales management team. Let me describe.

THE TEAM

Bill is not much of a numbers man. He doesn't like to keep records or keep score. He doesn't like it so much that he just plain doesn't do it. That is a problem. In some organizations, a weakness like Bill's could cause him a lot of grief. But Bill's agency realizes that what he is good at, what he's great at, is a rare and valuable commodity. So it only made sense to ask Sally, who is better at record keeping than Bill could ever hope to be, to do that part of Bill's sales management job. So that's what they did.

Another thing about Bill is he's a one-on-one wonder. It made him a top producer and makes him the coach of all sales coaches now. He's respected by both his seniors and his juniors because he's earned that respect and he mirrors it. Young guys like to work with him because he's a generously giving mentor. Older producers like him because he leads without lording it over them. He's willing to brainstorm, strategize, and riddle out a problem without putting his name all over it. Bill is the perfect sales coach and mentor. But in a classroom setting or a presentation in front of a group, Bill is just not very dynamic. He leaves them yawning every time.

The Wizard of Oz behind the curtain is the same one it is in most great agencies—Tom, the owner. Tom has the vision, the passion, the drive, the ambition, and the creativity. He puts on one of the best dog-and-pony shows you're ever likely to see. Tom is a mover and a shaker. He doesn't like to manage, but he's a great recruiter. Just don't let him be responsible for the actual hiring because he'll talk everyone into coming to work for him whether they can sell or not. If you ask him for advice, you'll probably get one of those stories, "Let me tell you about how I'd do it." So Tom asked Bill to do his sales coaching and mentoring and Bill asked Sally to manage his numbers.

It works! It works because the owner has created a culture that makes it easy to sell, makes it exciting to sell, makes it necessary to sell. That's how sales management can be practiced in the real world.

Successful sales management requires the practitioner(s) to perform at least four distinct and vital roles:

- Culture creator

  The visionary who establishes and maintains a strong sales culture

- Coach/mentor

  The person who coaches and mentors the sales team

- Product /project manager

  The one who provides strong product/project leadership and support

- Accountant/economist

  The individual who monitors and posts performance

Rarely, if ever, are all the different skill sets implied by these roles combined in a single person. In most agencies, one person performs one of these roles very well and a second one reasonably well. The other aspects of the job suffer in varying degrees, as does the sales effort. The following chart summarizes the personal attributes, responsibilities, and primary activities associated with each role.

Sharing the responsibilities of sales management within a team allows more individuals to earn recognition and respect for what they do best and allows the agency to meet all the demands of an active sales organization. The leadership challenge is to identify the best person for each essential role.

	Culture Creator	Coach/Mentor	Product/Project Manager	Accountant/ Economist
Answers the question . . .	What do we want to create? Who are we? What do we expect of our sales staff?	What is important to this producer personally & professionally? Where does he/she need coaching?	How can we differentiate ourselves in order to gain a clear advantage?	What is your level of activity & performance? Where will you be in three years if you maintain this pace?
Attributes	Recruiter, motivator, pacesetter, high visibility	Self-motivated, deflects personal glory, cooperative	Creative, productive, marketer	Logical, detail-oriented, able to define & obtain measurable data
Activities	Recruiting, speaking, opening doors	One-on-one coaching, training directing, sales calls	Discovers what clients want and responds with products & services	Collects, records, & reports monthly, quarterly, and annual results
Mismatch if . . .	Uncertain, no vision, poor presenter	Excessively competitive, poor listener, unorganized	Shallow, short-term thinker, lacks follow-through or initiative	Procrastinator, tunnel vision, impatient with details
Why . . .	People without vision perish. A business culture ties individuals together & gives a meaning & purpose to day-to-day working lives.	Most great performers have a coach to help them see what they cannot see. It's the fastest road to significant improvement.	Niche marketing is a proven road to business growth. A competitive market demands ongoing product development, which producers have neither the time nor expertise to provide.	You cannot chart a course if you don't know where you are, where you're going, & where you've been. Provides feedback, encourages healthy competitions, & focuses attention on goals.

We've developed a card game that has proven to be very useful in matching sales management styles. For more information on this sales management tool, go to www.thewedge.net.

THE WEDGE

Chapter 14
CRISP (Continuous Rapid Improvement Sales Process):
Sales Meetings of the Winners,
by the Winners, and for the Winners!

Winning isn't everything . . . it's the only thing.

– Vince Lombardi

When I ask owners and producers about their closing rates on proposals, I typically get answers ranging from 30-50 percent. When I ask the agency marketing staff, they generally say it's not that high. In many cases, no one really knows. There is no standard way to keep track. An industry journal calculated some time ago that the average closing rate was 18-22 percent. With such percentages, it's probable that a huge amount of overhead goes into activities that never bring a dime into the agency. Later in this chapter, you'll be given an exercise to help you determine what it really costs your agency to quote a piece of business. It might be an eye-opening experience.

When I first started working with agencies, it always confused me when someone said a new piece of business had to be on the books for three years before it started to become profitable to the agency. It wasn't until I started taking groups of agency owners through a cost-to-quote worksheet that combined hard and soft costs AND the closing percentage that I realized the cost of putting a new piece of business on the books. When you take into account those acquisition costs, commissions, and the cost to service the account, it starts to make sense. The only controllable factor in all of that is the acquisition cost. And the only way to reduce that is to increase the percentage of proposals that actually are closed. To do that, the focus needs to be on winning. So sales meetings of the winners, by the winners, and for the winners were born!

Not Another Sales Meeting

We've all played the role of Monday morning quarterback at sales meetings—second-guessing our team's mistakes, seeing that winning strategy when it's too late to change the outcome. Is it any wonder that everybody dreads them—even the sales manager?

Having had hundreds of opportunities in my career to be an outsider at a sales meeting, it's amazing to me how much time is spent attending and how little is gained. Instead, the sales meeting typically becomes a demoralizing public event or, at the very least, a complete waste of everybody's time—sometimes hours on end. As proof, many sales managers allow more seasoned veterans to skip them altogether, diluting the process even more. The worst part is when the sales meeting deteriorates into some kind of necessary evil, a kind of endurance training that most have decided—consciously or unconsciously—to live with instead of perceiving it as a problem to be solved.

Instead of staring through the rear view mirror, sales meeting should be about looking forward, acting with foresight, preparing to win before the whistle blows—when it counts. It should focus on sales. No, it *must* focus on sales.

Isn't Sales an Individual Sport?

One of my colleagues has a son who's a high school athlete. This year, he was part of a track team that had won the state championship four years straight. They were favorites to make it five. In case you're not familiar with track and field, scoring is gained in individual events and relays, which culminate in an overall team score—much like sales.

At their district meet, the unthinkable happened. In the 4 x 400 relay—an event they were a shoe-in to win—one runner misunderstood a judge's instruction, crossed over into lane one too soon, and the relay team was disqualified. Not only was it devastating to those four young men but to the team as a whole. In every previous year, that event had clinched the title. The winner of the 4 x 400 relay would claim twenty points in the overall score. And they were eliminated entirely.

Instead of admitting defeat and going after individual medals (like those schools that knew they had no chance of winning it all), they pulled together. They studied the individual times in each event for every school reaching the finals, made adjustments where possible to ensure their strengths would match up to the opposition's weaknesses, and decided that they would win it all together. Not only did they win their fifth straight team championship; they won more individual medals than they ever had in the past. The athletes who typically placed third or fourth rallied to have their best finishes ever. They won as individuals and as a team by working together.

To me, sales is just like that—working together to make use of every possible angle, edge, and strategy. Doing so will ensure both individual and team victories.

Well, Make it CRISP Then

My strong belief is that sales meetings are essential for maximizing success. To transform ineffective sales meetings into effective ones, they must be crisp and to the point. They must have a point, a purpose. From this, the CRISP sales meeting was born.

CRISP (Continuous and Rapid Improvement Sales Process) sales meetings have four distinct purposes, which become the outline or agenda for the meeting:

1. Getting introductions,

2. Setting new business appointments,

3. Submitting new business, and

4. Summarizing sales—so you can sellebrate!

Collectively, producers are the most valuable source of information. With CRISP, we collect that information and use it to empower the right producer at the right time with the right account. We use the power of the team to make each individual stronger.

I'll grant you, it doesn't happen overnight. And it doesn't happen without committed leadership from the top. Some new compensation rules will help drive the process. But I've seen it in small agencies and large ones. In small towns and big cities. In established agencies and newer ones. When your sales team comes together and works together, the success that results will blow your competition away.

CRISP sales meetings are held weekly or biweekly and typically include five to seven producers. They should be sixty-to-ninety minutes in length—no more, no less. The group size will ensure everyone's participation in this short period of time. If you have twenty-five producers, form four teams. Mix in newer and more seasoned producers, highly successful ones and strugglers. The mix helps everyone to grow stronger. Once the group is formed, it should remain stable.

One of the principal pitfalls in a team's success is allowing optional attendance. Attendance and accountability must be mandatory. Set the meeting schedule far enough in advance (same time every week) and accept no attendance excuses.

If possible, the team should meet in a room that is set up as your permanent war room. Your charts are posted there; your competitive files are housed there; your sales library and reference tools are available there. If your location must serve double-duty as a conference room for clients, one staff member should be responsible for updating charts and displaying them in the room prior to the start of each meeting.

The meeting's purpose is to create intimacy and ownership; to allow for free-flowing and, in many cases, challenging discussion; and to gain the value of several perspectives on a given situation or strategy.

The key objectives or priorities in a CRISP sales meeting are to:

- Leverage high quality relationships to get introductions.

- Maximize new business interviews with an effective precall strategy (including knowing critical details about the competition and prospect).

- Brainstorm approaches to business, including appropriate Wedges.

- Capitalize on the sales team, client base, and network to win business.

- Refuse to allow the weak to stay weak.

- Hold each other accountable.

For information on tools to set up your own war room, go to www.thewedge.net.

Identify It: Red Hot Introductions

Has your agency ever quoted on a piece of business that you didn't get only to discover later that someone else in your agency had a strong relationship with the business? I would bet that most of you have learned something after the fact that might have put a lost account in the win column. If you think it hasn't happened to you, you're probably wrong. The goal of Red Hot Introductions is to keep that from ever happening again by uncovering the information beforehand and using it to leverage and win new accounts.

In Chapter 15, we discuss in greater detail how every individual producer is separated from anyone he needs to know to close the next sale by only six degrees, six introductions. With CRISP, you have the opportunity to take the power and potential of your own inner circle and multiply that figure by five, or six, or seven—by all the members of your sales team. Each CRISP sales meeting begins with beginnings, with introductions. Why?

- Introduced customers generate more revenue than nonintroduced customers.

- Introduced customers cost the least to acquire.

- Introduced customers have a significantly higher retention rate.

Each producer is responsible for updating his introductions form.

CRISP Red Hot Introductions			
DATE	PRODUCER	SOURCE	INTRODUCTION

Use this form in your CRISP sales meetings in two ways. Add names of inner circle sources *and* enter the names of individuals to whom you need introductions. During the meeting, the goals for the sales leader are to:

- Stimulate the team to bring their prospects to the open table and use their collective resources (and sources) to find out who knows them or knows someone who knows them.

- Force individual producers to commit to asking for an introduction and a timeframe in which to obtain it.

- Enable support staff and coordinators to follow up and track results.

This is also the ideal time for your producer specialists to request introductions to current accounts in order to cross-sell additional product lines. With the owner of the current account as the introductory source, the same sales steps are followed:

- Develop the precall strategy prior to the interview.

- Complete the Five Principles of Prospecting prior to preparing a proposal.

- Project the closing odds and revenue estimate, then define the timeline.

Strategize It: New Business Interviews

Take your precall strategy (Chapter 16) to the next level—take it to the CRISP team. During the second part of your sales meeting, each producer has the unique opportunity to discuss an upcoming business interview with the team and mobilize the collective expertise to develop a strategy to win. By thoroughly analyzing an account, including uncovering potential obstacles, your producers will go into the interview prepared for almost any situation. No one should be caught off-guard.

Precall Strategy: Ask yourself and your team what critical information is needed before going into this interview:

- About this business and the individual players?

- About the competition—agent, agency, and carrier?

- About what we can bring to the table, our competitive advantage?

Wedges: The purpose of Wedges is to communicate competitive advantages. Prepare Wedges for several situations.

- Identify at least two proactive Wedges.

- Identify potential reactive Wedges.

- Create new Wedges for this specific situation.

Practice: No coach would use a game plan that his team hadn't practiced. Use your sales meeting as an opportunity to role-play and practice approaches.

Every CRISP new business interview appointment is logged and results tracked.

CRISP					
New Business Interview Appointments					
DATE	PRODUCER	COMPANY NAME	APPT.	X DATE	RESULT

The sales leader's goals are to:

- Exploit the power of the group to offer feedback, suggestions, and approaches to specific new business interviews.

- Develop best practice techniques to create a specific strategy for each individual sales interview.

- Improve the skill level of every producer through practice.

- Force producers to develop a predictable strategy for winning the account before they get to the interview.

Submit It: New Business Submissions

An introduction and an appointment do not necessarily equal one hot prospect. To increase your agency's batting average (not just your times at bat), you must make a deliberate decision to invest your time and resources only in those prospects that you can close. Major league hitters make split-second decisions about which pitches are worthwhile. They don't swing at every pitch, hoping to get a hit.

So why do sales professionals think every prospect is worth a submission? You too must learn to evaluate your prospects early enough in the game to cut your losses if the business is either not winnable or not worth winning. Stop fanning the catcher by swinging at every ball.

It's called qualifying the account. You define your ideal prospect. You make some decisions about size, business volume, location, and other criteria. You target the right accounts. As you go through the precall strategy with your colleagues, you get a better grip on the dynamics of the situation. So, by the time you meet your prospect face to face, you know you want to acquire this business. That's when you find out exactly what it is going to take to do that.

At the end of each new business interview you should be able to answer a series of no-nonsense, no-pooge questions that I call the Five Principles of Prospecting.

Did the prospect:

1. Tell you what your competitor wasn't doing?

2. Tell you that it was a problem?

3. Tell you what they wanted?

4. Invite you in?

5. Tell you they could fire the competitor and hire you if you bring them what they want?

If you have all the right answers, you are in a position to close the account. If your best take-aways and vision boxes did not secure an agent of record letter or an invitation to slay the incumbent, it is time to regroup, retool, or, perhaps, walk away.

We have groups we work with that are called Top Guns. They're all super producers who are serious about taking their sales game to a higher level. In one meeting, a young gun was having a hard time letting go of the fact that, if he didn't quote on the small, less desirable pieces of business that came his way, his competitors would. I asked, "Why wouldn't you want them to spend their time working on those prospects that take the most amount of time to service and bring in the least amount of profit? It gives you more time for your ideal prospect." At that point, he finally got it. You have to do things differently to get a different result.

Reviewing a less than stellar performance with your sales team can be tough. Just remember no one in the room wants anyone to fail. In a CRISP sales meeting everyone is trying to sharpen their skills, not their claws. This is the most supportive, collaborative audience you are likely to find. Like you, they are committed to continuous and rapid improvement.

These are the questions on which you and your team should focus:

- Where is the pain?

- How did you deal with the incumbent broker?

- What kind of commitment did you get in advance?

- How much revenue is in the deal?

- What are your chances of closing?

The sales manager can't afford to let producers waste time and money by quoting on accounts with little chance of closing. Your team should be open and honest with one other. If they are, everyone wins in the process.

As you review new business interviews in your CRISP meetings, you'll be completing this table.

CRISP NEW BUSINESS INTERVIEWS				
SUBMISSIONS	RENEW DATE	REVENUE	% PROB.	RESULT

The goals of the sales leader are to:

- Challenge producers to predict the likelihood of a sale before committing significant resources to a proposal.

- Work the Five Principles of Prospecting as a system for challenging those who are under prepared and over confident.

Quote It (or Not): The Cost of Quoting

As you go through the precall strategy, the relative difficulty or ease of closing a sale becomes apparent. But every new account extracts a cost in terms of time invested that needs to be justified by the dollar value of the account. What does it cost your agency to quote a piece of business?

You won't want to run cost-of-proposal calculations on every new account your agency pursues. But if you have never taken a pencil to the process, do it once. Complete the following table step by step. You might learn something eye-opening.

1. Estimate the revenue likely from an average-sized account.

2. Calculate the average annual compensation for a producer. Divide by 2,000 to get the hourly value of producer time. Estimate the number of hours projected in the activities involved in setting up the sale. Total the number of hours, multiply by the hourly producer value, and put that figure in Box #1, Producer Costs.

3. Define the average annual compensation for office or support staff and divide by 2,000. Estimate the number of hours of support time required for each activity listed. Total those hours, multiply the total by the hourly value, and put that figure in Box #2, Office Staff Costs

4. Calculate your average monthly overhead costs (rent, utilities, telephone, marketing expenses, business taxes,

profit sharing). Divide that number by 180, the number of work hours in a month. Multiply your average hourly overhead costs by the number of staff hours spent on the project and place that figure in Box #3, Overhead Costs. Estimate the total cost of supplies (printing/copying, paper, binders) and put that figure in Box #4, Supplies.

Total Boxes #1, 2, 3, and 4. Multiply that number by 4 (since closing ratios usually average around 25 percent). Insert that figure in the final box.

That is the Total Cost to Quote an average account for your agency.

COST OF QUOTE	
Producer average annual compensation $_____ ÷ 2,000 hours = _____ per hour	

PRODUCER COSTS	HOURS
Traveling to and from risk	
Meeting with introductory source, prospects	
Surveying risk	
Filling out application	
Preparing submission	
Reviewing quotes	
Following-up for additional information	

PRODUCER COSTS	HOURS
Developing proposal	
Presenting proposal	
TOTAL PRODUCER TIME	

Total producer time _____ x
producer hourly cost $ _____ = $ _____

1   PRODUCER COSTS $

Office staff average annual compensation $_____ ÷ 2,000
hours = _____ per hour

OFFICE/SUPPORT STAFF COSTS	HOURS
Preparing to quote	
Preparing submission/applications	
Receiving & reviewing quotes	
Preparing proposal	
Other	
TOTAL OFFICE/SUPPORT STAFF TIME	

Total office/support staff time _____ x office staff hourly cost
$ _____ = $ _____

2 OFFICE/SUPPORT STAFF COSTS $

Average monthly costs for overhead $_____ ÷
180 hours = _____ per hour

Average hourly overhead costs $_____ x
staff time _____ = $ _____

# 3	OVERHEAD	$
# 4	SUPPLIES	$
TOTAL COSTS: (#1 + #2 + #3 = #4)		$
Total Costs x 4 (average closing ratio of 25%)		$
TOTAL COST TO QUOTE		$

Win It: The CRISP Sales Summary

CRISP sales goals are team goals, not individual goals. Updating month-to-date sales figures at each meeting provides essential closure. Track business success in the most simple and direct way, by revenue of new business generated.

Add together the total annual new business revenue goal of each producer, then divide by twelve to calculate the team's monthly new business goal. As each new account is booked, it is added to the CRISP Sales Summary.

CRISP SALES SUMMARY Average Monthly Goal $ _____			
DATE	COMPANY	REVENUE	SUB-TOTAL

Sales leadership goals are to:

- Create a specific monthly goal for new business production.

- Compare the team goal to actual results on a monthly basis.

- Track progress by the only standard that matters, new business revenue.

Sellebrate It!

It's important to sellebrate your sales success—both as an individual and as a team. Post a sales banner and update it at each meeting. Recognize outstanding achievement. Provide financial incentives when possible. If that is not possible, reward your producers with something meaningful.

A CRISP Review

Using the CRISP process to prepare for and conduct sales meetings and putting The Wedge® tools in play during the meeting takes most of the fear and uncertainty out of sales. Better yet, you can put the FUN back in selling.

Here's the Short Course: For successful CRISP sales meetings keep the following tips in mind.

1. Create a permanent group of five-to-seven producers, no larger.

2. Meet weekly as an expected part of the sales culture routine.

3. Take advantage of the team atmosphere for both motivation and leadership.

4. The three most important goals are:

    •   To create accountability.

    •   To instill creativity, thinking outside the box.

    •   To track and encourage progress.

CRISP establishes routines and rituals that reinforce your company's vision and priorities and help to create a strong sales culture. Through CRISP sales meetings you can:

1. Set goals, priorities and performance standards

    •   Introductions

    •   New business interviews

    •   Submissions

    •   Most importantly—sales

2. Track progress

    •   Post CRISP charts in your war room or other public area

    •   Post new business goal banner prominently

3. Identify and practice skills

    •   Interviewing

    •   Wedges

    •   Presentations and closing

Setting a goal is not the main thing.

It is deciding how you will go about achieving it and staying with that plan.

- Tom Landry

Chapter 15
Red Hot Introductions

First is first, and second is nowhere.

– Ian Stewart

As a seasoned traveler, I usually get on the plane, close my eyes, and rest. I'm not that exhausted; it's my way of avoiding the dreadful conversation with the passenger the airline has placed way too close to me. One day to my surprise, I peeked through my fingers to see a perfect ten sitting next to me. Me! She—one of the most attractive women ever. I sneaked another look and was almost blinded by the glare of my wedding ring. All fantasies were immediately gone. But I struck up a conversation anyway. The more we talked about her and her interests, the more I realized that she and my brother (who is single) had a lot in common. Before we got off the plane, I got her business card. When I saw my brother the following day, I told him about the flight, the stunning woman I had sat next to, and how much they had a lot in common. I told him that I thought this was THE one and I couldn't wait to **refer** her to him!

Refer her?! You wouldn't refer one of the most interesting women you've ever met to your brother. You'd introduce them to each other. So would I.

That's the point. (In case you didn't think there was one to this shaggy dog story.) There's a huge difference between referrals and introductions. The same is true with your clients. They will introduce you to the other people they know all day long. But a referral seems both difficult to give and difficult for most people to ask for. The typical referral process goes something like this.

- "You know anyone who would benefit from the products and services we're providing you?"

- "Here's a card of a person I met. You can tell them I suggested you call."

For a Red Hot Intro script pocket card, just email us a request: contact@thewedge.net.

Typical Referral

As a producer, your first, most important, and greatest asset is your client base. Your current clients provide you with an annuity income year after year. Having serviced them well and socialized with them, you've built some great relationships. Yet, our experience with producers indicates that very, very few do an effective job of proactively and deliberately leveraging their client bases to be introduced into new prospects. Why not?

Three Reasons

There are three primary reasons. First and foremost, you like the annuity you receive from your accounts year after year. So the last thing you ever want to do is to stop that flow of money. Rather than risk jeopardizing the current relationship, you take a pass on asking for an introduction to the other business and social relationships your current clients have—forever.

The second reason piggybacks the first. You don't want to ask your clients for introductions because you really don't feel as if you deserve it. Why not? In your heart, you know you've done a good job for your client. But you also feel there is nothing unique or particularly outstanding about what you do. You write their insurance, they pay for it, you get a commission. You're thinking that the two of you are even.

The third and probably the biggest reason most producers never ask their clients for referrals or introductions is they don't want to look needy or greedy. Many producers are afraid that their clients are going to think, *if you're so darn professional and successful, why do you need help from me?* This kind of thinking will stop you cold in your tracks. As a result, you never ask for introductions or referrals.

The flip side of the third reason is that you truly don't want to look greedy. Some producers look at the client's modest clothes, modest car, and modest office and think, "I drive a new Lexus and belong to the country club; my kids are in private school. My service is good, but not extraordinary. I don't want to screw up this relationship by looking greedy. I'll pass now and wait for a better time."

Let's put these three reasons under a category called mental barriers. Until the mental barriers are gone, it doesn't matter if you know how to ask for introductions effectively or not, you'll never do it.

Two More Reasons

There are two more reasons producers don't leverage their client base for introductions. One very significant reason is that there is no good reason to ask. In other words, everything is fine. You have no real growth goals; your team has no vision. As a producer, you're making a decent living. You're probably growing your book of business by 3-7 percent every year. Your boss is content because he's making money. Your spouse is happy, too. When there is no compelling reason to ask, it doesn't happen.

The last reason is simple: you don't know how. You've never been taught how to ask for intros. Since you're comfortable making cold calls, you'll keep doing it.

Download the *Eliminate Mental Barriers* worksheet free from our Web site: www.thewedge.net/mb.

#1 at IBM

Jack Wilder is a friend from Dallas, Texas. When Big Blue (IBM) was the big dog back in the 70s, Jack was the number one salesperson twice. Put that in perspective. We're talking about one of the most successful companies on the planet at that time. Not only was IBM enormously successful and growing fast, they had an intense and competitive sales force. I asked Jack, "Are you that great as a salesperson?" He humbly said no, not really. I quizzed him on the secrets that led to such greatness. He said it was fairly simple. He identified the top twenty prospects within his territory, made a poster, and hung it on the outside of his office cube. More than 150 employees walked by every day, and each would glance at that poster. It was fairly common for someone to say, "I've got a friend who works at one of the companies on your list." Jack quickly would find out how well she knew the person and how strong the relationship was. If everything looked good, he'd be buying them all lunch as quickly as he could get it arranged. That's a Red Hot Introduction.

I've probably understated Jack's brilliance, intelligence, and selling skills. But Jack swore the one thing that put him over the top at IBM was his ability to leverage relationships and get in the doors of the businesses he wanted as clients.

Six Degrees of Separation

If you've ever bred dogs, six degrees of separation is one of your goals when selecting potential breeding pairs. To avoid inbreeding and encourage genetic diversity, you look for animals that have no shared ancestors in the past five generations. That's not what this is about.

The concept of Six Degrees of Separation is that you are only six connecting steps from anyone in the world (like the Kevin Bacon game, only bigger). It means you know someone, who knows someone, who knows someone, who knows someone, who knows someone anywhere in the world. Twelve years ago when I first heard this idea, I gave it a try to see how far I could go.

Here is my first test. I know Brian (state representative in Texas), who knew George W. (when he was governor of Texas), who knew his dad, George Bush (president of USA), who knew a lot of foreign heads of state and dignitaries, who know their countrymen. Bingo, I'm now somewhere in the middle of China, or South Africa, or the Court of St. James, meeting someone new.

The point is fairly simple. If I can get to China, through Brian, George W., and his dad, you can reach out and touch anyone in your city or region with a little thinking and planning. The reality is that you are only one or two degrees separated from almost anyone in your marketplace that you'd like to get to know. When you add your client base to those of all the other producers in your agency, it becomes a really small world. It makes prospecting bigger, better accounts a whole lot easier. You don't have to go in through the receptionist and personal assistant to get to talk to your prospect. You have an easier and more effective route.

Download the *Connect the Dots* worksheet free from out Web site: www.thewedge.net/cdot.

Imagine

So imagine this: you have eliminated the mental barriers that prevented you from asking for introductions. You also have a system to connect the dots on the relationship map. You know who knows whom. You're ready to implement a simple but elegant way to ask for introductions. Imagine sitting with one of your top twenty accounts. Having done your homework, you know to whom you want them to introduce you.

So you say, "John, you know Bill over at Texas Concrete don't you? Well, that's someone I want to meet. Would you be willing to set up lunch for us to get together?" With few exceptions, John will say, "I'd be happy to."

This creates your next challenge. What is John going to say to Bill to make him want to go to lunch with you? If John calls Bill and says, "I've got an insurance agent I want you to have lunch with. He's a nice guy and has done a good job for me.", is Bill going to want to meet you? Probably not. There's a pretty good chance that he already has an insurance agent who is a nice guy and does a pretty good job. Why does he need another one? You need a strategy to help John develop a compelling story so Bill will realize *there's something in it for him.*

Having worked with several thousand agents, I've asked them hundreds of times, how did you get that account? Too often the answer is relationship or timing. Seldom is it "We have a superior value proposition in the form of a proactive service timeline that includes specific services we provide that they didn't get from the incumbent agent. As a result, we keep our clients out of trouble, and they understand how we do it."

Obtaining a new account because you were able to develop a relationship over time is a good thing. Being at the right place at the right time and getting a new account also is a good thing. The difficult part about both relationship and timing is that they're unpredictable. Sales based upon a strong value proposition provides a very predictable flow of new business. Why is this so important when it comes to increasing the introductions you get?

As we stated above, the second and probably the biggest reason that agents don't consistently ask for and get introductions is that they don't believe they deserve them. If they did, they'd ask much more often. This same reason creates a problem for your introduction source. This source thinks of you as a good person who has taken care of his problems, but he knows that anyone worth his salt should have been able to do the same thing. And, the last thing he wants to do is embarrass himself by making a referral to a friend and have that friend say "I've got an agent, sounds a lot like yours. Let's just go play golf instead."

If any of this is hitting home with you, you'll also want to read the chapter on The Wedge®.

SODAR

Think of one of your clients who could be a great introduction source for you. Not only do you have a great relationship with this client, you also got him out of trouble when he needed you most. Of equal importance, you take care of his account on an ongoing basis by providing quarterly claim reviews, exposure analysis, and marketing strategies. You bring him renewal spreadsheets. Let's suppose you asked John, your client, to introduce you to Bill. How can you help prepare John to make a strong and powerful introduction, one that will get Bill's attention?

We use an acronym, SODAR. It could be the most power-ful tool in getting incredible Red Hot Introductions.

- Situation

- Opportunity

- Decision

- Action

- Result

The purpose of this technique is simple—to help your intro-duction source, John, tell a story so compelling that Bill wants to meet you because he *wants what you offer, not because he's doing John a favor.* You've got to prepare John. The best way to do that is use this acronym, SODAR, as a tool to remind you of the steps you want to take John through when developing his story for Bill.

SITUATION

The situation is simply what John's problem or situation was when you first met him. Example: experience mod was high, claims weren't being monitored, only saw agent at renewal.

OPPORTUNITY

The opportunity step is to help John remember how you came into the picture. Was it an introduction from someone else? Did you make a cold call? Had he seen you speak? Or had you just stayed in touch over a long period of time?

DECISION

The decision step is to help John remember what led up to his actually deciding to choose you. Did John call your refer-ences? Was it the style and completeness of your proposal? What pushed John over the edge to hire you?

ACTION

Since you were hired as the agent, what actions have you taken? Help John remember the ongoing proactive services you've provided to keep him out of trouble.

RESULT

Help John to quantify the results of your relationship. Quantify the dollars saved, quantify the time saved, quantify the worry eliminated. The key here is to help John recount a strong results-oriented story.

My business is not that much different than yours. Nobody needs a new sales-training program any more than they need a new agent. That's why I've got to help my introduction sources tell a compelling story that includes results. Here's an example of one that happened recently.

Situation: "We were closing a little more than 25 percent of our business. Average production was $50,000 per producer. Our sales meetings were boring, and there wasn't a lot of com- raderie in our sales team."

Opportunity: "I heard Randy speak recently at a conference and bought his book. After reading it, we got on the phone and talked."

Decision: "After having set goals for new business commis- sion and closing ratio, we developed a plan that we all bought into and signed a contract."

Action: "Our sales management team was trained in a sales- meeting format called CRISP. Then our producers were trained in The Wedge® and Red Hot Introductions. We also had review sessions every ninety days."

Result: "As a result, our new business commission has gone from $50,000 per producer to just over $97,000. Our closing ratio is now 81 percent, and we're getting over 70 percent of our new business by Agent of Record Letters."

Think about the power of SODAR. Getting your introduction source to search out and tell the whole story not only helps your source tell a compelling story that will get you in to your best prospects, it also helps retention. (How many of your good clients have amnesia? They forgot how bad it used to be, and they're wondering what you've done for them recently. This will help remedy that for a while.)

Put these together and you've got an endless supply of Red Hot Introductions. No more cold calls. No more waiting for the phone to ring. No more Rinky Dink Inc. referrals from which the commission wouldn't cover the gas it took to get to the bank and deposit the check—even if you sold the account.

How to Get Red Hot Introductions

1.   Think about who your existing client knows that you want to meet.

2.   Ask her if she would introduce you to that person.

3.   Take her through SODAR to develop the story.

4.   Ask her to make the call, tell the story, and set up lunch.

5.   Follow up.

This brief and simple process will help you shorten the time it takes for you to get into your best prospects, enabling you to start your precall strategy and win the business.

WEDGE

SECTION

4

The Flight Plan

The Flight Plan

Rule #1—Takeoffs must equal landings

Rule #2—Refer to Rule #1

Ironically, in a survey asking passengers of commercial airlines what was most important to them, the overwhelming response was to arrive on time. Safety was taken for granted, but arriving on time was not.

In the game of selling, most salespeople plan on failing 50-70 percent of the time. It's amazing how many salespeople see selling as a numbers game, not a game of quality processes leading to a quality outcome (getting paid). In sales, *arriving* at all isn't taken for granted; neither is safety.

We believe selling is like flying. If you don't land safely (and get paid), nothing else really matters. Getting attaboys for putting in hard work is nice, but it doesn't pay tuition to private schools. Commissions do.

Takeoffs must equal landings is the first rule you'll learn in flight school. At The Wedge® Flight School, the number one objective is to land and get paid.

Six major steps lead to many safe flights and a whole lot of money. Both are good.

Red Hot Introductions

If you were a pilot and wanted to make a trip, the first thing you would do is find a flight-worthy plane. You'd want a flying machine that could get you to your destination.

In sales the same is true. If I'm going to get paid, I better have a prospect that will get me to pay day successfully. If not, find one that will.

What's the best way to find a great prospect? It can be fairly simple if you have a client base. You could leverage that client base for introductions to great prospects. You learn more about that in Chapter 15.

Precall Strategy

Once you have that flight-worthy plane, you won't take off until you've filed a flight plan and done an instrument check to make sure everything is operating correctly.

The same should be true in sales. We call it a Precall Strategy. If you don't know who the competition is on your prospective account and you don't know who is going to influence the buy, you're going in half-cocked.

The great Michael Jordan once said, "For me to win, someone must lose." Jordan was great at understanding his competition, uncovering their weaknesses, and exploiting those weaknesses to win. You'll find out more about that in Chapter 16.

The Wedge ®

Unless you're a stunt pilot, you're not going to be comfortable flying at an altitude of 100 feet. It's dangerous and leaves little room for adjustments. The optimum altitude is about 30,000 feet if you're a commercial airliner.

The Wedge® is designed to help you gain altitude by

- Using differentiation to make the prospect dissatisfied and angry at the incumbent

- Finding out what the prospect really wants from an agent

- Determining if they can fire the incumbent and hire you

- If you can get those things working, you'll be flying high.

Keystone

Keystone is the equivalent of a smooth landing. You've been cleared; you're making your descent; your indicator lights show the landing gear is down. You're ready to land.

Every once in a while you land on your belly. The goal is to maintain control, stay alive, and not get hurt. You need a contingency plan.

Keystone is the process of getting permission to land the account and theoretically putting the wheels down—landing a new piece of profitable business.

Wedge-Proof

You've landed safely and are rolling toward the gate. You're parked. Wedge-proofing is strapping down the aircraft so it doesn't go anywhere in a storm. It ensures that once you've got a client, you keep him safe from snafus, second thoughts, and competitors who want to snatch him away.

Cross-Sell/Round-Out

You've landed, but it's a connecting flight. Even after you get your client safely to the first destination, there's more. Cross-sell and round-out is simply expanding the flight. The more business you have with a client, the less likely that she'll leave you. Make all your flights connecting ones.

Chapter 16

Precall Strategies: Forethought

You can't win them all—but you can try.

– Babe Didrikson Zaharias

Have you ever interviewed someone for a job at your firm, a CSR, marketing person, or another producer? Did any candidates hand you a resume and thank you for a chance to meet with you, then ask you to tell them about your firm? How long have you been in business? What are your products? Who do you sell to? At what point are you thinking, *you're wasting my time gathering information you should have already known? You're not here to win this job.*

Let's face it, if you walk into a prospect's office with only a business card and a grin, not knowing any of the firm's background, products, or size, you didn't do your homework. You're wasting the prospect's time and, within five minutes, he knows it. You are not even trying to win—and you probably won't.

Traditional Selling

On my bookshelf are more than 200 books on selling. Most of them will tell you that selling is a relationship business. Who could argue? Whether it's consultative selling, relationship selling, or high-trust selling, they're all telling you the same thing.

They say that there are two people in a sales interview, the seller and the buyer. They teach you to build a relationship with your prospect, find out her needs, meet her needs, and you should get paid. They never say anything about the third party at the table—the incumbent. As a result, the incumbent gets a last look at your proposal, a chance to match it, and, as often as not, the incumbent keeps the business.

Selling is about relationships, and the traditional selling models are half right. You do have to build a relationship with your prospect. But the other half of the process is that you have to break apart another relationship—the one between the prospect and the incumbent.

If you don't even know who the incumbent is, what he does, and how he does it, there's a real challenge. That's why you need a precall strategy.

Jordan's Rules

Michael Jordan is not only a great and gifted athlete; he is a fierce competitor. While playing professional basketball, his middle name was Winning. Two ideas characterized Jordan's desire to win.

Jordan knew:

- **His best had to be superior to everyone else's best.**

- **Someone had to lose for him to win.**

The precall strategy in selling is not much different from a flight plan in aviation or a game plan in sports. It is a basic part of the kind of planning that leads to winning.

Without a precall plan that requires you to learn who your competition is, you can never know how your best matches up to that of the competition. Is your best worse, equal, or superior to theirs? Without a precall plan how can you match your strengths against your competitor's weaknesses? How can you force them to lose so that you can win?

Nothing to Sell but Price

For an agency to survive and thrive, it has to bring in young talent and hope they have enough on the ball to survive the lean years.

It's not uncommon to bring in the young guy, help him get his license, then give him the yellow pages and tell him to start calling. If he's got enough drive to stay on the phone, he'll start to set a few appointments. Sooner or later, he'll get a chance to quote on an account. He'll get the policies from the prospect, fill out an application, send it to a few carriers, and get a price. If it's his lucky week, it'll be a great price. He'll present it to the buyer but won't be able to close on the spot. The incumbent will make his last minute presentation, find out he's high, call his underwriter, match the price, and keep the business.

Result? The rookie has a big fat ZERO next to his selling report, and the incumbent retained the account.

What does any of this have to do with precall planning? It goes back to the Jordan rules. My best has to be superior to everyone else's best, and someone has to lose for me to win.

Whether it's a rookie or a seasoned pro, the question is: what do you have to sell? The first clue comes from knowing who's on the account now.

Pro or Geek

If you look at agents, there are two extremes and those in the middle. One type of agent is the professional golfer with an insurance license. These are big on relationships but hand everything off to a CSR. The other extreme is the agent who loves insurance, to the point that he takes policies home for pleasure reading. "Hey honey, come look at how they worded this policy, isn't it clever?" The question I'm asking you to consider is, would you compete against these agents differently?

The other thing to consider is the agency. Some are basically a building housing twenty-to-thirty producers running around like headless chickens. There is no common way of doing business. There is no vision, no teamwork. You can bet they don't offer too many value-added services to their clients. On the other hand if you're competing with a regional firm, they could be very organized with in-house loss control, claims specialists, and HR services, as well as other points of service.

The question once again is, do you know your competition? Do you know what they do well and what they do poorly? If not, how will you develop an effective strategy to beat them?

In the Locker Room, It's Half Time

If you had a coach who didn't scout the competition, did not prepare a game plan, did not hold practice during the week but just asked every player to show up for the game and do his own thing—at what point would you think it's time to hire a replacement?

If your team goes out and plays the first half of the game, chances are good you'll be down by a few points. Then the coach brings everyone into the locker room and says, "Boys, we need to pull this one out. I want you to go play the best you can this second half and let's win!" The whole team is thinking, *what an idiot! If we had a game plan, we would have already kicked these guys in the head. We didn't even know whom we were playing!*

That's how most sales games are played. Show up and hope the first call goes well. Go back to the office and put together a second-half strategy and try to win.

A good precall strategy will get you off to the right start, enable you to find out who you are playing against (the competition), know more about how the referees make calls (the prospect), and put a winning team on the field. From the first kickoff, you must prepare to play and play with the absolute intention to win the game.

The Steps

In Chapter 14 on CRISP sales meetings, we discussed the importance of capitalizing on the experiences and knowledge of a small group to help strategize new business accounts. To prepare for that new account discussion, we suggested using a worksheet. Follow these steps to complete the worksheet for the meeting.

1. List name of company.

2. List all the buyers that will be involved in and influence the decision.

3. List the incumbent agent, agency, and carrier.

4. List the projected commission revenue generated from the account.

5. Answer the question, "What do you do that the incumbent agent does not?"

6. Answer the question, "Why does this prospect need you?"

7. List any outside sources that know the buyers and can help you gain an advantage

Precall planning exercises empower you to win new accounts by helping you develop a better understanding of your prospect before you show up. When you understand your competition's strengths and weaknesses, you can create and implement a plan to exploit them. You don't want the incumbent to have the upper hand. You don't want a level playing field. You want to turn everything possible to your advantage. If only one of you can win and the other has to lose, don't you want to be the winner?

WEDGE

CHAPTER 17
The Wedge®: How to Stop Selling and Start Winning

You do not merely want to be considered just the best of the best.

You want to be considered the only ones who do what you do.

– Jerry Garcia, The Grateful Dead

In my early days as a sales coach, I was working with three different agencies in the same area more or less simultaneously. On rare occasions, producers from each of the three agencies would be working on the same account. I learned a lot about sales working with those agencies.

In March of 1994, an account that we'll call Johnson Manufacturing was in play. John from the Alpha Agency was quoting on it, and so was Jim from the Beta Agency. I worked with each of these gentlemen on different days to develop the best strategy to sell the account. When we reviewed those accounts that had been won or lost sixty days later, Johnson Manufacturing came up. John from the Alpha Agency thought he had a good quote, but the incumbent agent Nancy had kept the account with a quote from Kemper. John suggested to the marketing department that the agency get appointed with Kemper since it was such a hot market. A few days later Jim from the Beta Agency had a similar story about how the incumbent kept the business with a great price.

Ironically, I had a meeting scheduled with the incumbent agent, Nancy. I congratulated Nancy on renewing her account and said I heard she had cleaned the other two producers' clocks. When she told me what really happened, it changed the way I looked at sales forever.

The Real Story

The whole situation was really quite different. The prospect told John and Jim that their prices were high and that's why they lost the business. In reality, both John and Jim had beaten Nancy's proposal significantly. However, Nancy asked for a chance to go back to her underwriter and see what she could do. The prospect gave her that chance.

After a hearty lunch and several of hours of schmoozing, the underwriter relented and matched the competing price. For Nancy, it was a dogfight—not at all the way the prospect painted the picture for the competing producers.

How often, I wondered, *does the prospect tell the competing producers they were high, when they actually had the best deal going in?*

If you were the buyer, why wouldn't you feed the competitor's price to the incumbent so she can match it? After all, once you get past the price issue, agencies and producers are pretty much the same.

The Value of Relationship

It became immediately apparent exactly how a relationship could be the ultimate sales tool in commercial insurance, whether it's property and casualty or employee benefits. Unless the incumbent screws up royally, there is a good chance she'll leverage her relationship to get a last look, the last quote, and keep the business. Somehow I had to help producers bust those incumbent relationships. As long as the incumbent was willing to work on retaining the business, the same old selling methods would never get the job done.

Reverse Engineering

We started at the end of the sales process and worked forward. We asked some pretty elementary questions, although it didn't seem that way at the time. We were trying to look at the process from the buyer's perspective. We put on our buyer's hat and asked the producer to make a sales call. Ask all the normal questions you'd ask on a sales call. From that exercise came the following, the Typical Sales Call.

THE TYPICAL SALES CALL

Producer: Mr. Jones, tell me about your business.

Prospect: We've been here seven years. We make widgets.

Producer: That's an interesting business. Are you the owner?

Prospect: Yes, I am.

Producer: Great. The reason I wanted to come by was to tell you about our agency and see if we could help you with any of your insurance problems.

Prospect: Fine.

Producer: We've been in business since 1942. We write lots of businesses like yours. We have great carriers and take pride in providing great service. Is there anything wrong with your current program that you'd like me to fix?

Prospect: No, nothing that I can think of.

Producer: Are you happy with your service?

Prospect: Yes. Everything seems to be fine.

Producer: Are you comfortable with the price you're paying?

Prospect: Oh, it seems fair. But insurance is expensive.

Producer: What I'd like to do is get a copy of your policies and see if I can improve on your coverage and lower your price. If I can do that, is there any reason why you wouldn't be able to make a change?

Prospect: Let's see what you can do and then we can talk about it.

Producer: Great! I'll just need copies of those policies and I'll get to work.

The producer will take this information back to the office, fill out an application, send it to the carrier, and wait to get a price to put in his proposal. At the sales meeting next week, the sales manager will ask the producer how the new business call went. The producer will tell him that the prospect had no problems and just wanted a better price. Everyone in the sales meeting will discuss the "fact" that all prospects are price buyers and no one cares about service anymore.

The price from the carrier looks good. With growing excitement, the producer puts together a professional presentation package with what he feels is a winning price proposal. He eagerly schedules another meeting with the prospect.

Producer: Thanks for letting me work on this for you. I think we've come up with something you're going to like.

The producer makes his presentation, showing the prospect where he found a gap in the coverage, which he closed, and how he also brought back a really competitive price.

Prospect: You sure know your business. You've done a great job and we're certainly going to consider you. Give me a few days to review my other bids and let's talk.

Producer: That sounds great. I'll call you on Friday.

When the producer returns to his office, the sales manager asks him how things went. The producer tells him that the meeting went very well. He feels that he has the best package and that he's developed good rapport with the prospect. If they get it, and he hopes they will, he'll know Friday.

Friday comes, but the anticipated phone call does not. Late in the afternoon, the producer finally calls the prospect. The prospect has already left for the day. The producer spends the weekend wondering if he got the deal. Monday morning the prospect returns his call.

Producer: I suppose you've made a decision. How did we do?

Prospect: You were real competitive and did an excellent job. I was impressed with your professionalism. Unfortunately, the difference between your pricing and my current agent's just wasn't enough to justify a move. Thanks for your efforts. I'd really like you to stay in touch and work on it again next year.

Producer: I'll do that. I'd like to get your business and I know
             with a little more time we can develop an even bet-
             ter program for you.

The producer makes a notation to call the prospect in nine
months. At the next sales meeting, the producer says, "We got
beat on price again. I think we should work hard on upgrading
our marketing efforts and the carriers we do business with.
We're getting beat on price a lot!" What really happened was he
got rolled. The reality is that he can save the prospect money
and improve coverage, but the incumbent leveraged his relationship to get the last look, matched the price, and kept the
business. It happens all the time.

That's the typical sales call. In all too many cases, the
prospect is giving you an opportunity to quote just to "keep the
incumbent honest." Your quote is meant to confirm that the
prospect is already getting a fair market price. If the incumbent's pricing is too high, the prospect can then use your proposal to pressure the current agent into cutting his rate in order
to keep the account. That's one big reason why incumbent
agents enjoy a 92 percent retention rate in commercial lines;
they have a relationship and leverage it to get the last look.

Selling is Easy Compared to Buying

To buyers, insurance is a commodity. When we surveyed
agencies from across the country about how they differentiated
themselves from their competitors, they named the following
so-called unique features.

	Reputation	Representation	Great Technicians	Risk Management	Loss Control Services	Claim Services	Years in Business	Customer Service	Competitive Pricing
COMPETITOR #1	❏	❏	❏	❏	❏	❏	❏	❏	❏
COMPETITOR #2	❏	❏	❏	❏	❏	❏	❏	❏	❏
COMPETITOR #3	❏	❏	❏	❏	❏	❏	❏	❏	❏
COMPETITOR #4	❏	❏	❏	❏	❏	❏	❏	❏	❏
COMPETITOR #5	❏	❏	❏	❏	❏	❏	❏	❏	❏
COMPETITOR #6	❏	❏	❏	❏	❏	❏	❏	❏	❏

Look familiar? Obviously, touting the things that you think make you different could actually make you sound very much the same.

From the buyer's perspective, nine out of ten agencies had the same value proposition. Agents wanted to get the policies, check for coverage gaps, select a carrier, and see if they could save the prospect money. If all agents were primarily doing the same thing the decision was easy. The buyer could pick almost any agent and do fine. There just wasn't that much difference.

So the number one task to improve sales was to create discernable areas of differentiation that could be clearly and simply communicated.

We began by dividing the business of selling insurance into three sections—price, coverage, and service. It seemed to us that price was a factor of *last one in wins*. Coverage was something that many agents already did very well. So we focused on service. We looked at service in two ways—reactive service and proactive service.

Two Kinds of Service

Reactive service can be described as the ability to respond to a client's needs. If the client calls, do you return the call? Can you get certificates and endorsements out on time? Can you get the policies delivered in a reasonable time? If the client has a claim, can you respond promptly and help solve the problem? Most agencies do a good job of responding to their clients' needs. Those that didn't are out of business. You could define most agency service cultures as reactive service cultures that were developed to retain clients by responding to their imminent needs.

Proactive service—that was scheduled in advance and delivered not in response to a request or problem but to *prevent* problems from happening—was almost nonexistent.

The lesson was simple. Don't compete on price. The incumbent will get the last look and match it. Don't compete on coverage. The incumbent will get a chance to negotiate the same coverage with his carrier and keep the business. Don't compete on service. Most prospects hear the word service and assume you mean you'll respond to their requests. They get that now and they expect it from you. After all, from the buyer's point of view, that's what they're paying for.

To win you have to compete in an area where your competition is weak and you are strong. Your competitors are reasonably strong at price, coverage, and reactive service. But they're not very strong in the area of proactive service, so that's where you can beat them.

Don't Say They Didn't

We helped our agents develop a proactive service timeline. It included a number of possible services: claims reviews; x-mod worksheets; payroll review; business income worksheets; certificate review; and other options.

Now we had two initial problems. First, if we told the prospect we could do all of these wonderful things for them, they would nod and say "That's great, put it in your proposal." In the meantime, they would take our ideas and ask the incumbent if they could do the same things. The incumbent would certainly say yes. Oops, there goes our advantage.

Our next strategy was to get them to see that the incumbent had been taking advantage of them by asking, "Did your agent do a quarterly claims review?" The problem was that the prospect quickly got defensive when we asked it that way.

Our solution was to develop an approach that assumes the prospect is already getting this from the agent even though we don't think he is. That way he won't get defensive but will start to question the quality of service the incumbent is providing. So we tried a question like this:

"When your agent comes out ninety days after renewal to do a claims review—review the loss runs, locate the reserves that are too high, and get them reduced so you don't have to overpay for your workers comp insurance—are you comfortable with how they go through that process?"

Bingo. It worked. The prospect clearly understood what should have happened but hadn't. He didn't get defensive but instead felt the incumbent was underserving him. Ouch! We had found the pain.

Five Steps of The Wedge®

The way to create an opportunity is to drive a wedge between the client and incumbent agent.

STEP ONE: PICTURE PERFECT

Service failures can be painfully obvious. But omissions, even significant ones, are invisible to the prospect. If you can provide value-added services to the prospect, you can also gain a strategic advantage. You must make the prospect feel and acknowledge pain in his current business relationship. Man is a pleasure-seeking/pain-avoiding animal, but pain has the upper hand. Unless he feels the hurt, the law of inertia will take over and everything will stay in place—including you on the outside looking in.

"**When** your current agent **came out** after ninety days **to** review your loss runs together **so that** you could adjust your reserves, were you able to identify claims with high reserves? Are you starting to get a handle on that now?"

The prospect responds, "Well no. We've never actually done that. Should we?"

To which you respond, "Well, it's not that big a deal if you feel the insurance company is looking out for your best interest."

That is a Wedge—the thin edge of doubt and dissatisfaction. Additional wedges will increase the pain and widen the gap between your prospect and the incumbent agent. To create a Wedge, complete a simple recipe card by filling in the essential ingredients.

Step Two: The Take-Away

Once the client understands the benefit of your proactive service, he must confirm that its absence is a problem. Examine your proactive service from the point of view of the customer so that you can educate your prospect on the penalties (pain) that could result if tha t particular service is *taken away*.

SUBJECT		BENEFIT		TROUBLE
Claims Review	>	lower reserves	>	high modifier/ overpay

Based on the benefit and potential trouble, outline a take-away script.

PICTURE PERFECT	SOFTENING STATEMENT	TAKE-AWAY	TRANSITION	EMOTIONAL HOOK
Claims review	(shrug) I don't know	Maybe it's not that important	because	the carrier would never set the reserve too high. You'll never have that high a modifier

Step Three: Vision Box

The Vision Box is a method for getting the prospect to tell you what he wants from an agent—in his own words, as if it were his own idea.

Involve the prospect in expanding his vision of the claims review process. Begin by sharing a story of another client company that went through a very successful claims review process. Explain how many people from various areas of responsibility were involved in the review, how long it lasted, what issues they focused on, how follow-up was handled, and what results were achieved. Now you are ready to help your prospect plan for his own claims review session.

Vision Box

Who

How   **What**

Why   **When**

Where

When: When do you want to schedule this?

Who: Whom would you like to have at the meeting? Who
            will be involved in the follow-up?

What: What role do you want to play? Do you want the
            loss runs in advance? What do you want to accomplish during the meeting? What do you want done
            afterwards as follow-up?

Where: What's the best place to meet?

How: How long should the meeting be? How long should
            the whole process, start to finish, take? Do we want
            to look at every claim or focus on those over a certain dollar amount?

Why: Why will this benefit you?

Both you and your prospect are invested in the process
now.

STEP FOUR: THE REPLAY

Together you have created a Vision Box that incorporates a comprehensive proactive service timeline. You want to review that timeline and *replay* the prospect's decision that he really wants all of these things to happen on the agreed schedule. Mirror the vision your prospect has created back to him. It is crucial that you avoid using the words I or me as you describe the plan. Make sure that he hears his own words, his own plan, coming from your mouth. Ask him to confirm that this is exactly what he wants and expects from his insurance provider. Once your prospect is emotionally committed to a plan, fall on your sword.

STEP FIVE: WHITE FLAG

Ask him what he would like you to do. Give him control. To gain leverage, never ask for the sale. Make him ask you. Getting invited in gives you the leverage to deal with the prospect's ability to fire the incumbent agent and hire you.

It may help to visualize the entire process as a continuum.

PICTURE PERFECT	TAKE-AWAY	TRAN-SITION	VISION BOX	THIRD-PARTY STORY	REPLAY	WHITE FLAG
Claims Review	It may not be that important because the carrier would never set the reserves too high.	Can we talk about that?	What would you like to have happen?	One company like yours wanted (who, what, when where, why & how). Does that make sense to you? Which parts?	Here's what I'm hearing you say you want. Anything else?	Okay, so what would you like me to do next?

A Palace Coup

So he waves the white flag. He asks you to submit a proposal. *Can you help us?* He begs or confesses *I'd like to see this happen.* If you accept an invitation to quote on the business and leave now, you will be rolled. If your opponent, the incumbent, gets an opportunity to match your price and match your promises, you lose. The incumbent can promise anything (perhaps over Scotch and water) and win. He is not really obliged to deliver. He doesn't need to. He's already in.

On the other hand, you have your foot wedged in the door. You have inserted a gap between the prospect and his agent. You have a unique opportunity to drive The Wedge® through the incumbent's heart and win this account. It goes something like this.

You: I'd love to give you a proposal that includes all the things we've talked about so that you can really get some control over your insurance issues. But that could create a real problem for you.

Prospect: What kind of problem?

You: Suppose it's three weeks from now and here I am again. This time I have a proposal in my hands that includes everything we've talked about—your *must haves* and your *nice to haves*. As soon as you read it and see the figures, you know this could make a real difference to your firm, to the bottom line, and to your day-in day-out routine. Can you imagine that?

Prospect: I'm imagining.

You: Even as you're looking at the proposal, you're saying to yourself: *This is it! We've found ourselves a new agent.* Now you're on the horns of a dilemma. I'm wondering, can we deal with that?

Prospect: What's the dilemma?

You: Well, when you decide to make this change, some-
             one has to tell your old agent. How are you going to
             tell him that it's over?

Prospect: Hummm. I hadn't thought about that.

The not-so secret about The Wedge® is that you have been
in competition from day one with the incumbent AND the
prospect's ability to fire the incumbent. If he hasn't got the
authority or the will to do the dirty deed, you don't have a
prospect. There is no potential account. You made the term
great service meaningful to the prospect by expanding his vision
box so that he could see himself doing business with you. Now
you must take the sting out of firing the incumbent by taking
the prospect through the event in advance.

Prospect: Hummm. I hadn't thought about that.

You: Well, I can tell you right now what will happen
             when your agent hears you're going to make a
             change. He'll rush over and say everything he can
             think of to convince you to leave things just where
             they are. When that happens, how are you going to
             handle that?

Prospect: I'll just have to tell him that business is business.

You: Can you do it?

Prospect: Sure.

You: And when he comes in with a wine and cheese bas-
             ket, and pours you a glass of the good stuff and
             says, please don't do this to me. How will you han-
             dle that?

Prospect: Do you think he'd really do that?

You: He has a family, and a mortgage, and car payments
             just like you and I do. You'll be an important client
             for me. Yours has got to be a big account for him.
             He'll do anything, say anything, promise anything
             to hang onto you. When he shows up, how are you
             going to handle it?

Prospect: I'm ready to make a change. And I can explain that
             to him.

You: Can you do it?

Prospect: Absolutely. Not a problem.

You: Then I'll get started on that proposal.

    Now, the deal is closed.

    This rehearsal technique will help the prospect deal with
the issues on an intellectual level. If the incumbent has not performed the services you've described, the client has every right
to feel painfully underserviced. He has rationalized the pain (all
insurance agents are the same) and emotionalized his relationship with the incumbent. By talking him through the painful
experience of firing the incumbent, he can remove the emotion
from the situation and act more rationally in this business situation. You've also given the prospect an important opportunity
to let off emotional steam. He has gained control over the situation, has time to anticipate and prepare for the incumbent's
responses, and will develop the confidence to take charge.

Five Steps of The Wedge®

1. Picture Perfect

2. Take-away

3. Vision Box

4. Replay

5. White Flag

Conclusion

This chapter is a book in itself, not coincidentally called *The Wedge*®. It is also a seminar for top producers and those who want to be and a video-training program.

Chapter 18

Keystone: Locking the Deal in Place

Winning is not a sometime thing; it's an all time thing. You don't win once in a while,

You don't do things right once in a while, you do them right all the time.

Winning is a habit. Unfortunately, so is losing.

– Vince Lombardi

Would someone please tell me, when is the sale made? When you get a check?

There are lots of opinions about when the sale is made. Mine has always been that the sale is made up front. It's made on the first or second interview. Seldom is it really made at the closing interview. It's made when you get a Red Hot Introduction; when you Wedge out the incumbent and rehearse your prospect's telling the other guy it's over. It's made when your prospect tells you what he doesn't like about the incumbent (picture perfect); what he really wants (vision box); confirms it (replay); invites you into the game (white flag); and rehearses firing the incumbent agent. As a matter of fact, I can introduce you to hundreds of producers who are doing this and getting AOR/BOR letters right up front. So when is the sale made? Hopefully the sale is made early in the game, but what happens when it isn't?

When the sale isn't made up front, you need something to lock it up. That's why we call this step of the selling process Keystone. If you were a Roman stonemason two thousand years ago, you would have mastered the engineering miracle of the Roman arch. The Roman arch begins with two pillars upon which stones are placed in such a way that they gradually step upward and inward, toward the opposite pillar. The arch is capped by a single central stone with a characteristic wedge shape—the keystone. The keystone locks the other stones in place. The weight of all the stones on the left pillar presses against the left side of the keystone while the pressure of the stones atop the right pillar pushes against the right side of the keystone. Without the keystone, everything would collapse. It holds the two forces in balance, creating an opening that is both beautiful and stable.

Murphy's Law

Murphy said, "Anything that can go wrong, probably will." Was Murphy a pessimist, a realist, or just from Boston? (Go ahead—make a joke about Texas.) The good news about Murphy is that he planned for the worst. As a result, he was prepared to turn his lemons into lemonade.

If you did a good job on the first call and got the agreement that the prospect could fire the incumbent and hire you, you should have a high closing ratio. The Keystone process will just help you nail it down and deal with the hiccups that can happen at closing time.

Developing Your Options

Let's imagine that your proposal and the incumbent's quote are both on the table. Let's take it for granted that you're always going to be in the game with your coverage. The other two components are price and service. Keep in mind that when we talk about service, we are talking about proactive service, not just reacting or responding when your client has a need. The three scenarios are:

1. You have the best price and better service.

2. You have the same price and better service.

3. You have a higher price and better service.

If you don't have better service, then you don't need this chapter. If your primary game is to match coverage and save money then you either need to read Chapter 17 on The Wedge® again or just skip this part and do a Best Deal Close.

Looking at Your Options

OPTION ONE

You have the best price and better service. When that happens, you want to know what your prospect is going to do:

1. Buy from you

2. Give the incumbent another shot.

OPTION TWO

You have the same price and better service. What happens then? Is your prospect going to go with you to get the better service, or will he be overcome with guilt since you didn't save him any money and stay with the incumbent?

OPTION THREE

You have the higher price but better service. Are you dead in the water or can you work a BOR?

The purpose of this chapter is to get you to think through your options under each scenario and plan offensive and defensive strategies.

Keystone: Six Steps to Lock Your Deal in Place

1. **Greeting.** Break the ice, establish rapport, get comfortable.

2. **Future Pace.** Tell them what's going to happen over the next forty-five minutes. Suggest that you believe they are going to like and want your proposal.

3. **Rehearsal.** Confirm that when they get what they want, they *still* have the ability to fire the incumbent and hire you.

4. **Present Service.** Outline and underscore the items in your proposal that are the same as what they have had before and the proactive service that is different.

5. **Present Coverage.** Review the details of the coverage, limits, and exclusions

6. **Determine Action.** Find out what direction your prospect is going to take.

   a. Hire you

   b. Defer decision

   c. Give the incumbent last look

GREETING

You know how to greet people by now. If not, you'll enjoy the book *Instant Rapport* by Michael Brooks (Warner Books

1990). You'll also learn some great ways to make people comfortable.

FUTURE PACE

In about five minutes, you'll have read this chapter. At that point, you probably will say to yourself, *this makes a lot of sense. I need to customize this for my own situation.* The thing is, your time is limited to get it done. When you hit that time roadblock, how are you going to handle it?

That, ladies and gentlemen, is an example of Future Pace. You simply take your prospect into the future and get her to imagine what she is going to do. The Keystone process recommends that you do the same. Tell her that you have her proposal. You might use an analogy like the following one to demonstrate the difference between your proposal and the normal proposal.

Example: This proposal is like a car. One section has all the basics you expect—the wheels, engine, tires, and chassis. This section, however, has all the customized features like the special sound systems, radar detector, and Global Positioning System. When we get through this proposal, I think you're going to say, "Yes, this is exactly what I want." At that point it's going to create the dilemma that we discussed sixty days ago. How will you deal with the other guy?

REHEARSAL

If you followed The Wedge® process the way it was designed, you took your prospect through the rehearsal technique when you first met with her. Now it's time to review it again and make sure that your prospect is still willing and able to fire the incumbent when she gets what she wants. You want to make sure that nothing has changed. The key here is not to wimp out. The danger is that you've done all the heavy lifting and, if you're not careful, the prospect could give you a weak answer like, "Let's cross that bridge when we get there." If you're not strong, you're on your way to getting rolled.

PRESENT SERVICE AND COVERAGE PROPOSAL

Hopefully, you've developed a written service timeline with the events that will take place over the next twelve months. You've detailed who will be involved, when it will happen, and what the results will be. Get agreement that it matches up with what your prospect wants. When the service proposal is complete, go through your coverage proposal with coverage, limits, exclusions, and pricing.

DETERMINE ACTION

This is where the poop hits the fan. As we discussed earlier, one of three things will happen. You will have the best price and best service. You will have same price and best service. Or you will have the highest price and best service. When you finish presenting your service, coverage, and price proposal you might say, "There it is. You've got two options now. You could tell me right now to get started. Is that what you want?" You might be surprised how often you will get a yes if you've done all the steps well. However, often the prospect will tell you he still has another proposal. If that's the case, here is where you really earn your money. It's time to stop, rewind, and replay the Future Pace technique.

If the incumbent will be offered an opportunity to submit a revised quote, ask if you can, in fairness, have the same courtesy. Point out the foolishness of an endless cycle of quotes and ask for a commitment to hold fast to initial submissions on the agreed date.

If it is clear that any pricing differential will sink the deal, get confirmation that the additional services you are providing have a tangible value. Since he has already affirmed to you that he wants these services and they are important to him, ask him to put a dollar value on them or explain how he could obtain these same services with current staffing and budget. Work to get a commitment that your additional services have a dollar value equal to a percentage (10-15 percent) of the contract pricing.

If it is apparent that the carrier selection is heavily impacting the pricing, get agreement that he will allow you to serve as the agency of record with the current carrier.

Because this can get confusing, I suggest you write it out just like the illustration.

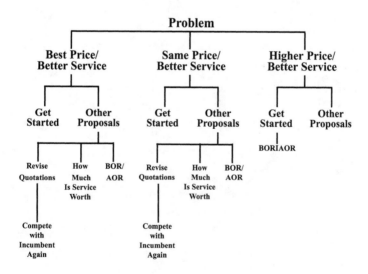

When all is said and done, the winner is generally the one who is best prepared. Keystone helps you prepare to close the deal. It's the last piece that locks the deal in place.

WEDGE

CHAPTER 19

Wedgeproofing and Cross-Selling Your Accounts

Begin at the beginning and go on till you come to the end; then stop.

– Lewis Carroll

Even Superman was vulnerable to the enemy when kryptonite was around. I remember one exciting episode in which he had just enough power to rip a lead pipe out of the wall, stuff the kryptonite in the pipe, and crush each end with his bare hands, sealing off the krypto just in time to regain his energy and keep his superpower. You don't want to have to be superman to retain your accounts.

A, B, C. One, two, three. Use the kindergarten method of Wedgeproofing your accounts. First you start by defining your A, B, and C accounts.

A ACCOUNTS

Your largest accounts that generate 20 percent of your revenue.

B Accounts

Your next tier of accounts that contribute 40 percent of your revenue.

C Accounts

All the accounts that collectively make up the bottom 40 percent of your revenue.

Second, you decide one, two, and three. In other words, how many times a year are you going to visit your A accounts? Three times? How about your B accounts? Two times a year? Finally, your C accounts? Probably one time to renew the account.

Perhaps this is a bit oversimplified, but compare it to the chaos that exists now. More than likely you, as a producer, or your firm have big accounts that get very little proactive service and many smaller accounts that are service intensive. Does that mean that the big accounts are vulnerable and smaller accounts are over serviced? Could be. So the simplest way to Wedgeproof your accounts is to set up a standard service calendar with real proactive service that keeps your client out of trouble, eliminates surprises, and brings real value.

Cross-Sell

The other way to Wedgeproof your account, improve account retention, and increase revenue is to cross-sell. Some firms are great at this and some aren't. The biggest obstacle to cross-selling is a willing producer. There are some agencies in which cross-selling is the norm and a company-wide goal. There are others in which cross-selling never has happened and never will. But there are many agencies in which cross-selling is optional. If the producers want to, they can. If they don't, they don't have to.

So the key to cross-selling is first to find a willing producer. Second, go back to Chapter 16 on precall strategy and use those techniques to develop the information needed to win. Equally important is getting the producer to make a Red Hot Introduction (see Chapter 15). If you have a problem with producers wanting to cross-sell go all the way back to Chapter 2 on vision to determine if it's really important enough. If it is and it's one of your strategies to grow the agency, your next stop is Chapter 14 on CRISP sales meetings.

The most successful agencies write all or nearly all the insurance business for their key accounts. It is one of the most effective ways to solidify the relationship between client and agency. In small agencies, this leads to more frequent contacts and a stronger relationship between a single producer and customer service representative and the client company. In a larger organization, it means that multiple agency representatives are developing relationships with several key personnel within the client company. Either way, it is a win-win situation. It is more effective, more efficient, and less expensive for the agency to maintain the account. The ultimate goal of The Wedge® is to develop such a strong relationship between agency and client that they function as partners, frequently partners for life.

WEDGE

SECTION

5

The Million Dollar Producer

The Million Dollar Producer

I have brought you to the ring, now you must dance.

– Robert the Bruce

Can everyone become million dollar producers? They probably can; they just won't. Why not? Start with: my town is too small; the accounts are too small; buyers only buy price; it's too much responsibility; the agency holds me back; I can't find a good CSR; and there's too much competition. These are all good reasons and there are lots more.

There are only two reasons you'll become a Million Dollar Producer. One is you absolutely want it. The other is that it'll be given to you. I can't control your bloodline, but I can help fortify your desire, develop your plan, teach you winning processes, and improve your execution.

This section could be subtitled *How to Double Your Book in Three Years with Half as Many Accounts.* Think about it. If you do that a couple of times, mathematics will work in your favor. You (or anyone) could have a million-dollar book.

Thousands of producers have $200,000-$400,000 books of business. It's only taken them twenty years to grow it, which means they're averaging $10,000-$20,000 growth per year. If you're satisfied with that growth level, you don't need this section. Just continue to work a little harder each year.

Million Dollar Producers function like a company within the company, a sales culture within the larger corporate culture. All the same factors are there:

- environment

- vision

- goals and priorities

- routines and habits

- ceremonies

- cultural network

By bringing all these elements together into a workable plan, you can get there from where you are. So if your dream is to be a Million Dollar Producer, turn the page.

Chapter 20

Vision Too: Seeing in Seven Figures

*One does not discover new lands without consenting to
lose sight of the shore for a very long time.*

– Andre Gide

To grow an agency, you have to have vision. To be a Million Dollar Producer, you have to have Vision Too

When Tiger Woods was ten years old, he taped a picture of Jack Nicklaus to his headboard, envisioning that one day he'd be as good, even better. Eleven years later, Tiger won the Masters by twelve strokes. Although Tiger won, he knew he didn't have the swing that would make him better than his idol. So he told his coach that he wanted to rebuild his swing. Tiger was cautioned that results would not come overnight. It would take weeks of training to develop stronger forearms and months to groove in his new swing; his tournament play would get worse before it got better.

Mechanically, Tiger would drastically rotate his hips and shoulders on his downswing to create his monstrous tee shot. But sometimes his arms couldn't keep up with the rest of his body and he'd yank one into the rough. Tiger's coach restricted his hips and slowed the rotation of his torso on the downswing. He also adjusted his grip. The plan was that, as Tiger's forearms strengthened, he would be able to address the ball squarely on impact and produce a more consistently straight shot.

Woods only won one tour event during the next nineteen months. It frustrated and angered him to be playing out of the rough where his shots often landed. But each time he lost, he declared he was a better golfer.

The rest is history. His vision, planning, practice, and execution paid off. He won an extraordinary ten of fourteen events in 1999.

If you want to be a Million Dollar Producer, you have to have Vision Too. Bet on it. You're going to get worse before you get better. You'll probably say, "Look where I am now. Why should I change?" Each time you do, read the story about Tiger one more time.

Vision

Let's talk about your vision. Suppose it's three years from now and you and I are having a cup of coffee. You tell me that the past three years have been one great run for you. So great, in fact, that you're celebrating your initiation into the Million Dollar Club! What would have had to happen during those three years for you to sit and tell me that?

Life, business, and sports are played on many different levels. When you've finally made it to the top of one level, you're at the bottom of another one. And what's really interesting is that what got you to the top of the first level won't get you to the top of the next. It takes new skills, habits, or ways of doing business. Tiger Woods was absolutely at the top of one level. But he was at the bottom of the next.

THE WALL

When Tiger realized he couldn't get to the next level without significant change, he was at the wall. Many producers are there as well. Are you at the top of your game, producing at a level that puts you at the top of your agency? So is that enough for you?

There is a Japanese term, *Kaizen*. It has no English equivalent. Kaizen means constant and never-ending improvement. Making changes, tinkering with success, usually results in a temporary worsening of the situation. The fear is that things won't improve, that change is too risky. When fear creeps in, instead of making the change, many people justify status quo as being good enough. Many, but not all. People who never heard the word Kaizen are on their own never-ending missions to grow and improve themselves. Eighty-year-olds can and do go to college. Mother Teresa never retired. Nor has Bill Gates. Gates actually has become more deeply involved in the R & D aspects of his business as time goes on. Many, if not most, artists, writers, composers, and geniuses of all sorts continue to create and invent all their lives, all the way to the grave, even though their reputations are secure.

Your Kaizen and your vision are crucial to growing a million dollar book of business.

ZONES

My daughter Reagan, who is four years old, wanted to learn to play baseball like her older sisters. We started out on the lowest level, pitch and catch. I showed her how to hold her glove out in front of her to catch the ball. My first pitch was a little too high and a little too hard. The ball hit her on the shoulder and she got a little stinger. She immediately threw down the glove and started crying. Reagan was in the red zone of playing pitch and catch. Red zone means she was a *don't know how*. She didn't know how to catch. But fortunately for me, her vision of being like her sisters is strong and powerful. She hung in there and we kept playing. She put out her glove. I tossed the ball into the glove and it stayed there. She didn't really catch it, but she didn't drop it either. That's the yellow zone. At this point, she's a *know about*. That means she pretends that she can catch. After a few hours of play over the next several days, Reagan finally got to where she could catch the ball. It was great! I would throw it and she'd put her glove in the right place and squeeze. Now she's in the green zone of that game.

Of course, kids are never satisfied. Now Reagan wants to play baseball in the front yard with the other kids. That's a bigger game. There are more people, and she'll have to learn to bat and run the bases. New game means new red zone, and the cycle begins again.

Anytime you move up to a bigger game you're going to go through the zones—red, yellow, and green. Red zone is a *don't know how* area. Tiger Woods hired Butch Harmon to help him rebuild his swing because he didn't know how. For nineteen months, Tiger didn't win a tournament. He was playing from the yellow zone. Then one day, things began to click. He felt it happening. His swing felt natural again—green zone.

Believing in the Vision Too

If you want to be a Million Dollar Producer, you need vision. Your vision, like Tiger's and little Reagan's, has to be powerful enough to get you through the stingers and the setbacks. Do you have a role model? Can you conjure up a picture of what your career and life could be like if you moved up to the next level and joined the hallowed ranks of Million Dollar Producers? Do you believe?

Where do our beliefs come from anyway? From within. We learn from experience—ours and others. But more importantly, we interpret those experiences. Our interpretations then form the basis of belief. You've heard the story about the brothers who grew up in New York's Hells Kitchen. One becomes a criminal and the other a priest. Same genetics. Same upbringing. Two radically different interpretations of life. One finds meaning and hope all around him. One sees none. One believes he can rise above everything. The other doesn't, can't, and won't.

Have you ever seen someone you admired interviewed on television? The usual question is, how did she do it? The usual answer is a series of steps or actions. *First this happened and I did that. And then* . . . Very few interviewers or subjects begin at the beginning. "I had a belief that I could. . . ." Sometimes the subject backs into the idea by talking about what her grandmother always told her. But usually, we never discover that kernel of belief that leads, almost inevitably, to success. We seldom ask and seldom learn why some people simply believe that the impossible really is possible. No wonder we attribute so much to luck. It makes it so much easier for us to blame our shortcomings on bad luck, or bad timing, or just being in the wrong place at the wrong time.

Where did Roger Bannister ever get the idea back in 1954 that it was possible for a human being to run a mile in less than four minutes? We may never know. But he believed that he could break the four-minute barrier and that's exactly what he did. The following year, thirty-seven separate individuals followed his lead and did the same. A year after that, there were 300. Once the world's runners, coaches, and trainers believed that breaking the mythical, magical four-minute mark was no longer a barrier, but a goal, it became universally possible.

So what makes you believe that good enough is good enough? What experiences in your life; what observations of life around you; what failures, losses, disappointments, and embarrassments have you interpreted to mean that where you are is pretty much as far as you can go? Tough questions. But if you can take one of your own self-limiting beliefs and truly, honestly examine how and why you came to hold that belief, you're on the road to wellness.

Beliefs have been compared to a table, supported not by a single interpretation but by several. The tabletop of some beliefs is as flimsy as a folding card table, supported by feeble-legged notions like "something I read back in junior high school." Others are substantial, six- and eight-legged structures with supports more on the order of "I tried it. I fell flat on my face. It hurt like blue blazes and cost me a promotion." Jack enough tables-of-belief up on enough legs and pretty soon, you've built yourself a ceiling. Now where are you going to grow?

You *can* change the beliefs that are holding you down. How? Pain. The fastest way to change a behavior or belief is through pain. Think back to the steps of creating a Wedge. Find the pain. Failing that, create the pain. What pain does your negative belief cause you? How much does it hurt? Will the painful consequences escalate with time? What if your threshold for pain suddenly drops? What if you just can't take it any more? Begin to associate anything with pain (remembering psychic pain can be far more intense than real pain), and you *will* change it.

You also have the ability to selectively replace your negative, self-limiting beliefs with positive, empowering ones. No one else does. But if you will inventory your most empowering and your most self-defeating beliefs, you'll quickly see which ones need work. We may build our own ceilings, but we can also build our own ladders.

Once you have a vision in which you can believe, you must act. Your vision will compel you to act. You'll need some bigger, bolder strategies. You'll want a system to give you more quality time—time devoted to pursuing your goals. And as you and your priorities change, your relationships also will evolve. You'll want to manage that process too. The next two chapters are about creating those strategies, refocusing your time, and developing the relationships that will make you a Million Dollar Producer.

WEDGE

Chapter 21

Me, Inc.

A ship in the harbor is safe.

But that's not what ships are built for.

– Anonymous

S ome professionals—like doctors and attorneys—automatically see themselves as corporations. So do Million Dollar Producers. Me, Inc., is your own growing enterprise within the larger agency. You are the president and CEO. You have the vision. You're chasing that big seven-figure goal. Next you need a strategic plan to make sure you get there.

Pinpointing Your Future Needs

One way to get more fuel in your rocket is to simply schedule out your major financial needs for the next twenty years. Whether you're single or married, with or without kids, you have some major financial needs coming at some point in the future. It was a little scary for me to do this, but it brought home the truth about my future financial needs. With four daughters that are two, four, six, and eight, it doesn't take a genius to figure out that major expenses like braces, cars, college, and weddings are just over the horizon. That doesn't include all the minor, but significant, expenses like camps and proms.

Before you get started, I can tell you countless numbers of stories about highly paid professionals who had kids that would someday be college bound yet did not save for that major event. As a result, it put them in a financial bind for at least six to eight years as they worked to pay college tuition out of the monthly cash flow. It meant hard times for many. Why suffer that fate when you can plan for it now by increasing your earnings and investing that additional revenue over time?

Turn to the Tools section at the end of the book and do **Pinpointing Your Future Needs** exercise. Do not proceed until you finish the exercise.

Now that you've determined how much money you want to make, let's calculate how much business you have to write to get there.

Turn to the Tools section and fill out the **Producer Income Goal Sheet**. Do not go until you've finished this worksheet.

We began with your vision to become a Million Dollar Producer. Then you looked twenty years out to identify and quantify your major financial needs. Afterwards you planned your income for the next twelve months by determining how much new business you'll have to write to earn that amount of money. Now let's develop a strategy to get there.

Me, Inc., Strategic Plan

First, let's analyze your account mix. Pareto's Principle or the 80/20 rule states that 80 percent of your revenues are generated by 20 percent of your accounts.

Conversely, 80 percent of your agency's time is spent servicing the bottom 20 percent of its accounts. You can readily assess the value of your accounts in terms of revenue. But because the CSRs' salaries, phone and express mail bills, computer time, disruptions to other business, and miscellaneous supplies are not deducted from your commission check, the cost of servicing that account is largely hidden. When evaluating the relative value of your accounts, consider the following factors in the total cost of service:

- time

- energy

- problems

- expenses

- employees

Without any doubt, your agency and Me, Inc., are subsidizing a large number of your accounts with the revenues generated by others. What to do? This conundrum is what is known in scientific circles as a *No Brainer*. Change your mix.

Rebalance your account portfolio by eliminating those accounts that eat your time and feed you poorly. You can:

- Convert them to house accounts,

- Enhance a new producer's book with accounts that are too small for your book but just right for her,

- Continue to maintain the accounts, but make the decision not to renew, or

- Maintain as a house account, do not renew, AND encourage the client to consider one of your competitors.

Your goal should be to convert the bottom 80 percent of your book within the next thirty-six months, replacing those poorly producing accounts with fewer but better accounts. How you proceed toward that goal will depend on your market and your book. Like most of your goals, it is a three-year process. Producers who are determined to redirect their careers will cut fairly deep, fairly quickly. If you land a really plum account, you might even decide to eliminate all 80 percent in the first year. Pace yourself, but don't procrastinate.

In the Tools section you will find a system to help you analyze the relative value of your current accounts.

THE AGENCY VERSUS ME, INC.

Not every agency owner is going to be thrilled by your new initiatives. Your fellow producers might think you want to skim the cream from the whole dang marketplace. Of course, you do. But if five $400,000 producers became Million Dollar Producers in three years—where would that put the agency? Bottom line: expect some resistance.

You are taking your game to another level. And the game is played a little differently up there. Prepare your case for why you need the best CSRs and more CSRs. Your whole team may need additional training so its members can fill bigger shoes. Those proactive services you're planning to use to Wedge out the competition? They've got to be created first. That takes time and resources. You may need faster computers or a glitzier presentation package. You must position yourself and your team to win.

THE ME, INC., TEAM

It takes a village—or at least a team—to raise a million-dollar book. The Million Dollar Producer, like Tiger Woods, is not really an individual. He's an entourage. Dan Sullivan, known as the strategic coach, said, "You can't make $100,000 a year doing

$12 per hour work." Your time and energy must be refocused on developing new accounts, new initiatives, new markets, new resources. That means you *must* get out of the reactive business and delegate those responsibilities.

You absolutely, positively, definitely, unequivocally, and conclusively cannot be the person who responds to client service needs. That is what your CSRs are hired and trained to do. Most of the time if you, the producer, stayed out of the way, the CSR would handle the service request better and faster. You should not even hear about a service glitch unless it escalates to an incident. Reactive situations should not involve you, and you should not involve yourself in them.

Your role is a proactive one. The proactive services you offer your clients have real and measurable value to them. By providing these proactive services on a regular schedule, you are positioning yourself as a professional resource instead of a service technician. Your value to the client thereby increases, making it easier for you to leverage the account for introductions and cross-selling opportunities.

As you are upgrading the nature of your client interactions, you also are becoming the leader of your new team. Polish those managing, mentoring, and leadership skills. Lay the groundwork for successful relationships between your team members and your clients by introducing them to one another. Provide or initiate training. As Me, Inc., takes off, you may need to recruit an account manager or prepare a trusted CSR for that level of responsibility. In short, part of growing a successful business is successfully growing the support staff.

As you read through this chapter, it must all seem so simple, so elementary. In fact, it's so obvious, you're probably asking yourself why you haven't developed and executed such a plan long before now. Maybe it's your bucket.

The Bucket

Imagine that your book of business is like a five-gallon bucket. In the bottom of your bucket are the accounts that you write now. Let's suppose that taken together these accounts are equal to one gallon of water. You still have four gallons of capacity—theoretically.

STEP 1

The first step necessary to grow your book of business is to create a vision of how big you want it to be and let that drive your revenue goal. That done, it's time to go to work. That means, go write new business.

STEP 2

Writing new business begins with developing your Top 20 Prospect List so that you can leverage your existing client base for Red Hot Introductions to these and other prospects.

This is generally where the trouble begins. You're out of time. Initially you burn a little midnight oil, give up weekends for a while, and work a lot harder. But you soon discover that, like *Alice Through the Looking Glass,* it takes all the running you can do just to stand in place. Once you realize that you can't run any faster or work any harder, you realize something is wrong with this equation.

STEP 3

About now you discover that the reason you are out of time and cannot run any faster is that you have holes in your bucket. Time, energy, and revenue are leaking out as fast as you put more in. You'll have to plug the holes in the bucket to free up time and energy. Those holes represent several things: 1) low payoff activities, 2) routine service items you have been trapped into doing, and 3) poor systems and processes that force you to constantly create and recreate.

STEP 4

When you try to focus on building new business relationships, you find yourself trapped, anchored, attached to your old bucket. You can never let go. Those holes are caused by:

1. too many small accounts, and

2. the inability to delegate routine service items.

That is why you need a plan such as the one we outlined to:

1. analyze and adjust your account mix, and

2. create systems to delegate more service items.

If you're not careful, you'll never escape the bucket long enough to develop the relationships you need to accomplish your goals.

At this point in the evolution of Me, Inc., we've discussed the agency environment, your vision, your goals, your strategic plan, and your team or cultural network. If you're ready to grow into the role, the responsibilities, and the revenue of a Million Dollar Producer, the next chapter will help you to develop routines, habits, and ceremonies that prioritize your time and activities so you stay on track.

WEDGE

Chapter 22
Twenty/20

What's talked about

Is a dream.

What's envisioned

Is exciting.

What's planned

Becomes possible.

What's scheduled

Becomes real.

– T. Robbins

Get real. To become a Million Dollar Producer, the first thing you have to do is start acting like one. Unless you are exceptional indeed, you're going to need to reshuffle your deck—do things differently, use your time differently, do some different things. It's a whole new routine.

Twenty/20

We know. Prospecting and closing new accounts is hard work. That's why they pay you the big bucks to do it. It's a lot easier to service established accounts. That's why it's such an easy trap to fall in to. You can't afford to backslide, wool-gather, or lollygag if you want to join the Million Dollar Club. To keep yourself moving forward, put yourself on a Twenty/20 Program.

Begin with your 20 Day Game Plan (see form at the end of this book). You play the game by earning Million Dollar Producer (MDP) points. At the rate of twenty MDP points a week, you win by accumulating eighty MDP points over the course of the twenty working days of the month. To help you, a MDP Point Key is located at the end of the book.

Clearly, some activities carry more weight. These are the activities that carry you toward your goal. Filling your time with low point activities might make you look busy around the office, but you'll never win the big game that way.

TOP 20 PERCENT ACCOUNTS

They're keepers—that top 20 percent of your current accounts. So by all means, you want to keep them. That's why each of your key accounts should be on a proactive service timeline (see Chapter 17 on The Wedge®). In theory, your time-line will put you face-to-face with your best clients every other month—not to solve service problems or react to the crisis *du jour*. These meetings are scheduled in advance to provide a value-added professional service. It's service that requires some advance preparation by you and your team. And it's a priority item on your agenda. As you acquire bigger, better accounts, your list of keeper clients will grow as will your schedule of Proactive Service Timelines to execute. Remember, if everything goes as planned, your entire book will be primo accounts—the creme de la creme. Keeping up with the keepers is going to become an ever-expanding part of your job.

TOP 20 PROSPECTS

You probably already have a Top 20 Prospect List. Get it out. Look at it—hard. From a Million Dollar Producer's vision, are these still your top twenty prospects? The Top 20 Form at the end of this book will help you to quantify and qualify your Top 20 Prospects by prompting you to fill in the blanks—the estimated revenue value of the account, the renewal date, the carrier, the incumbent agency/agent. What have you done to get closer to closing these accounts lately? The form helps you track and focus your efforts.

TOP 20 INTRONET

Getting Red Hot Introductions (see Chapter 15) is a crucial part of your twenty-day game plan. The people (clients, colleagues, and others) you ask for introductions and the people (prospects) to whom you want to be introduced are your intronet. The Top 20 Intronet form at the end of this book will help you monitor your progress on both fronts.

All of our Million Dollar Producer forms can be provided to you in electronic format, ready to load onto your laptop. Just e-mail us at forms@thewedge.net.

Ceremonies and Sellebrations!

Don't forget to sellebrate. Let me say that again, don't forget to sellebrate—with your team, with your colleagues. All those wonderful ceremonies of success—the wall charts, the banners, the wheels of fortune, and the atta boys that drive the vision for the agency should be adapted for Me, Inc., in order to maintain high motivation and low turnover on your team.

Maybe you need to develop a Me, Inc., mini-CRISP meeting—a quick, ten-minute, every-man-standing, flash of a meeting to reinforce the bond and keep everyone on target. You certainly need a birthday tradition, an anniversary acknowledgment, and an above-and-beyond-the-call reward.

Don't forget to maintain clear boundaries between what is yours, mine, and the agency's. Sometimes the cost of such events is expensed. Sometimes, it's your treat. And sometimes staff members really want to split the tab, take up a collection for gifts, or bring homemade cakes and covered dishes so that they can feel part of the process.

I have a young nephew who built himself a dance club and bar in a rust-bucket former steel town in northern Ohio. When I visited him at his place of business, he offered me a beer. I watched as he took three dollars out of his wallet and put them in the till. "I thought you owned the joint," I said.

"I do," he replied. "Even though 40 percent of every dollar in there is mine, I decided early on that it's better to buy someone a drink than to give them a drink. It has more value to them that way." I thought then that he was a young man wise beyond his years.

In Conclusion

I hope you have just paused, rested your open book on your chest and sighed. I hope the ideas that you've just read about have inspired you to dream bigger than you have ever dared to dream. I hope you've come to realize that if you can dream it, you can do it. YOU CAN DO IT! I've tried to outline a system and some simple processes that demonstrate how you can focus energy on the dream and the doing of the dream.

So what are you waiting for? Get growing.

SECTION

6

Breaking the Sales Barrier Tools

Pinpointing Your Future Needs

Insert Total Dollars Needed Each Year

	retirement				parental care				weddings				college				autos				mortgage			
	1	2	3	4	1	2	3	4	1	2	3	4	1	2	3	4	1	2	3	4	1	2	3	4

Insert Age

ANNUAL INDIVIDUAL GOALS FOR

ANNUAL

1. **Personal Income Goal**

2. **Less Guaranteed Income**
   (Book $ x Retention % x Renewal %)

3. **New Personal Income Needed**
   (Line 1 - Line 2)

4. **New Revenue**
   (Divide Line 3 by Line 1 to Determine New Revenue%)

5. **Average Commission per Sale**

6. **New Sales Needed**
   (Divide Line 3 by Line 5 to determine number of New Sales Needed)

7. **Closing Ratio**

8. **Submissions Ratio____%
   Submissions Needed**
   (Line 6 divided by closing ratio%)

9. **Interview Ratio____%
   New Business Interviews Needed**
   (Line 8 divided by Submissions Ratio%)

10. **Intros Needed**
    (Line 9 divided by Interview Ratio%)

Analyze Your Book of Business

Stat Section

A. Book of Business
(Gross Renewable Commission) _____

B. Commission Rate for Renewal Business _____

C. Commission Rate for New Business _____

D. Interview Ratio
(Introductions to Interviews) _____

E. Submission Ratio
(Interviews to Submissions) _____

F. Closing Ratio
(Submissions to Close) _____

G. Retention Rate _____
(% Of Gross Commission Renewal / % Total Book of Business)

Analyze Your Accounts Using the Attached Worksheet

1. List your accounts from largest to smallest on the attached work-sheet

2. Add up the total number of accounts and multiply by 20%
   - Example: 150 accounts X 20% (150X.20=30)

3. Identify the top 20%
   - Go back to your list of accounts, listed from largest to smallest.
   - Identify your top 30 accounts – that is who you really want to service

4. Identify the bottom 20%
   - Go back to your list of accounts, listed from largest to smallest.
   - Identify your bottom 30 accounts – that is who want to get rid of

Analyzing Your Book of Business

Account Name	Commission

4 POINT DAY for Million Dollar Producers

POINTS

1   Getting an Introduction to a Decision Maker

1   Cross-Selling an Established Account

2   Getting an Appointment to Meet with a Decision Maker

2   Meeting with a Key Account to Provide a Proactive Service

3   Meeting the Decision Maker of a Prospective Account Face-to-Face

4   Getting a Commitment to Close or an Action that Directly Leads to Closing the Account

20 Day Game Plan

				Monthly Total

Top 20 Prospects

Account Name	# of Prod.	# Loc	E.B. Date	Revenue	Cur. Prog.	Jan	Feb	Mar	Apr	May	Jun	Jul	Aug	Sep	Oct	Nov	Dec

M=Mail   V=Visit   P=Phone

The Wedge® Group @ 877-999-9334 or www.thewedge.net

Top 20 Intronet

Intro Source	Intro Company	Jan	Feb	Mar	Apr	May	Jun	Jul	Aug	Sep	Oct	Nov	Dec

ABOUT THE AUTHORS

Randy Schwantz, author of *The Wedge: How to Stop Selling and Start Winning* and coauthor of *Breaking The Sales Barrier: How to Develop Million Dollar Producers,* creates and delivers thought-provoking presentations that connect with every member of an audience. He brings a passion and belief to his work that immediately engages seminar participants. He has been called inspiring, provoking, and even outrageous.

Randy has been a successful salesperson for more than twenty years. However, a little over ten years ago his primary interest became the sales process itself. He began to work closely with producers and sales leaders of all kinds, spending thousands of hours in sales meetings and in one-on-one coaching sessions, as well as attending countless workshops and seminars.

Randy's mission is threefold. His primary goal is to change the way producers prospect and sell—to help them be more successful and fulfilled. Second, he continues to work closely with sales leaders and producers as coach and consultant. Finally, he believes there is always something more to be learned about the sales process. He continues to study and to meet with colleagues and producers to develop and improve future programs.

On the personal side, Randy is married and has four daughters. They live on The Wedge® Ranch in Argyle, Texas. A bit of a daredevil, he's participated in—and lived to tell about—firewalking, skydiving, parasailing, and improv comedy. He has received his master certification in neuro-linguistic programming.

Brian Jenkins is a seasoned trainer and presenter whose fast-paced style is heavy on information and motivation and short on boredom. His no-fluff style is crisp, clean, and to the point.

After attending Louisiana State University on a football scholarship, Brian spent the better part of a decade as a businessowner. He launched a commercial cleaning franchise company in Miami. After nine months and phenomenal growth, he parlayed his success in Miami into the Chicago market. Within eighteen months, the Chicago operations tripled. This dramatic growth in Chicago and Miami funded new operations in Houston. Within seven years, Brian's start-up venture had multiplied into 250 franchises.

Brian, coauthor of *Breaking The Sales Barrier: How to Develop Million Dollar Producers* is the COO and vice president of sales and marketing for The Wedge® Group. His goal is to help organizations create a sales culture. By transferring simple techniques to company leadership as well as training individuals, the sales culture becomes seamless even as new employees are hired or acquisitions are made.

On the personal side, Brian, his wife, and three children make their home in Keller, Texas. When he's not enjoying a game of golf or a pick-up game of basketball, he might be whitewater rafting down the Zambizi River in Africa or on a wildlife safari.

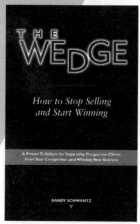

Need Additional Copies?

Call 1-800-543-0874 to order and ask for operator BB or fax your order to 1-800-874-1916. Order on the web at www.nationalunderwriter.com. Ask about our complete line of products.

PAYMENT INFORMATION

Add shipping & handling charges to all orders as indicated. If your order exceeds total amount listed in chart, call 1-800-543-0874 for shipping & handling charge. Any order of 10 or more or $250.00 or over will be billed for shipping by actual weight, plus a handling fee. Unconditional 30 day guarantee.

SHIPPING & HANDLING (Additional)

Order Total	Shipping & handling
$20.00 to $39.99	$6.00
40.00 to 59.99	7.00
60.00 to 79.99	9.00
80.00 to 109.99	10.00
110.00 to 149.99	12.00
150.00 to 199.99	13.00
200.00 to 249.99	15.50

Shipping and handling rates for the continental U.S. only. Call 1-800-543-0874 for overseas rates.

SALES TAX
(Additional)

Sales tax is required for residents of the following states:

CA, DC, FL, GA, IL, KY, NJ, NY, OH, PA, WA.

The
NATIONAL
UNDERWRITER
Company
PROFESSIONAL PUBLISHING GROUP

Orders Dept #2-BB
P.O. Box 14448 · Cincinnati, OH 45250-9786

2-BB

_____ Copies of *Breaking the Sales Barrier* (#4220000) $31.95

❑ Check enclosed*   ❑ Charge my VISA/MC/AmEx (circle one)

*Make check payable to The National Underwriter Company. Please include the appropriate shipping & handling charges and any applicable sales tax.

Card # _____ Exp. Date _____

Signature _____

Name _____ Title _____

Company _____

Street Address _____

City _____ State _____ Zip _____

Business Phone (_____) _____ Fax (_____) _____

E-mail_____

The
NATIONAL
UNDERWRITER
Company
PROFESSIONAL PUBLISHING GROUP

Orders Dept #2-BB
P.O. Box 14448 · Cincinnati, OH 45250-9786

2-BB

_____ Copies of *Breaking the Sales Barrier* (#4220000) $31.95

❑ Check enclosed*   ❑ Charge my VISA/MC/AmEx (circle one)

*Make check payable to The National Underwriter Company. Please include the appropriate shipping & handling charges and any applicable sales tax.

Card # _____ Exp. Date _____

Signature _____

Name _____ Title _____

Company _____

Street Address _____

City _____ State _____ Zip _____

Business Phone (_____) _____ Fax (_____) _____

E-mail_____

BUSINESS REPLY MAIL
FIRST CLASS MAIL   PERMIT NO 68   CINCINNATI, OH

POSTAGE WILL BE PAID BY ADDRESSEE

The National Underwriter Co.
Orders Department #2-BB
P.O. Box 14448
Cincinnati, OH 45250-9786

NO POSTAGE
NECESSARY
IF MAILED
IN THE
UNITED STATES

BUSINESS REPLY MAIL
FIRST CLASS MAIL   PERMIT NO 68   CINCINNATI, OH

POSTAGE WILL BE PAID BY ADDRESSEE

The National Underwriter Co.
Orders Department #2-BB
P.O. Box 14448
Cincinnati, OH 45250-9786